NAVIGATING
motherhood

A PRACTICAL GUIDE FOR EVERY DAY MUMS

MAVEN PRESS

Copyright © Laura Elizabeth
First published in Australia in 2022
by Maven Press
Roleystone WA 6111

Cover Design by Adrianna Grosso

Edited by Jade Bell

All rights reserved. No part of this book may be used or reproduced by any means, graphic, electronic, or mechanical, including photocopying, recording, taping or by any information storage retrieval system without the written permission of the copyright owner except in the case of brief quotations embodied in critical articles and reviews.

Because of the dynamic nature of the Internet, any web addresses or links contained in this book may have changed since publication and may no longer be vaild. The views expressed in this work are solely those of the author and do not necessarily reflect the views of the publisher and the publisher hereby disclaims any responsibility for them.

 A catalogue record for this work is available from the National Library of Australia

National Library of Australia Catalogue-in-Publication data:
Navigatinig Motherhood: A Practical Guide For Every Day Mums/Laura Elizabeth

ISBN: 978-0-6456356-0-7
(Paperback)

ISBN: 978-0-6456356-1-4
(Ebook)

Acknowledgements

In unity, we honour and pay our respects to the custodians of Whadjuk Noongar Boodjar country, the lands on which this book was first seeded.

We pay our respects to the Elders both past and present and to those emerging.

The stories within these pages may contain sensitive content and/or memories of loved ones who have passed on, which may activate a response within you.

Please read with awareness and care.

Contents

Shani-Faye Chambers
INTRODUCTION 1

Ash Moreland
YOU MATTER TOO 3

Aimee Brown
MAKING HEALTH SIMPLE 13

Marilou Coombe
NAVIGATING THE JOURNEY 24

Diana Welch
EXPECTATIONS VERSUS REALITY 33

Sarah Holroyd Hill
THE REBIRTH 42

Aasta Ryan
CONNECTION AS SELF-CARE 49

Shani-Faye Chambers
CO-PARENTING WITH GRACE 58

Maryanne Sayers
SLEEP – THE ULTIMATE INGREDIENT..................................67

Kara Williams
CULTIVATING HEALTHY HABITS 77

Kelly Lam
ALIGN YOUR LIFE...86

Nathalie Biviano
NURTURING YOUR MARRIAGE 96

Kelly Kilah
SELF-CARE REQIURES BALANCE....................................106

Leticia Corrina
THE ENERGETIC SHIFT..115

Kate Hamilton
PERFECTION – YOU'VE ALREADY ACHIEVED IT............125

Amy Campbell
IMPOSTER SYNDROME 134

Lisa Smith
PREPARING FOR PARENTHOOD 142

Nina Cruz
FINDING YOUR MAGIC IN MOTHERHOOD......................155

Shani-Faye Chambers
Introduction

I see you, Mama. All you, Mamas. The single mamas, the married mamas, the working mums and the stay-at-home mums, the mamas looking after the children with special needs, and the mamas whose partners are more like children than husbands.

No matter your age, your background or the level of support you do or don't have, we're all navigating the same challenges, learning how to honour and take care of ourselves while being responsible for raising our babes.

Is it pretty easy to forget about ourselves in all this, right? Whether it's the crying baby, teenagers going through hardship, disagreements with the father on parenting styles or just the very talkative five-year-old who you swear doesn't breathe between the constant chattering and stories that lead nowhere. So where is the space for us in all of that?

They say motherhood is the most challenging and rewarding 'job' you'll ever do. And it is. Because every day, every phase and every year of their life, we're met with new challenges. Add extra siblings, issues with your partner or a troublesome mother-in-law to the equation, and suddenly you''re experiencing new dynamics and challenges. Then, just when you think you got it all figured out? It all suddenly changes.

Personally, I think the key to navigating Motherhood, isn't about trying not to lose ourselves but learning how to reinvent ourselves—learning how to be the most loving, kind and understanding mother to ourselves first. And Learning that amongst it all, you are the one that needs and deserves the most compassion from yourself.

I also think it's helpful to realise we are not alone in our struggles. Billions of women before us and billions of women after us will experience the exact same emotions, worries, situations and concerns. There is no shame in our experiences, and only healing and wisdom are to be gained by sharing them. It's time to realise you are not alone, Mama, and regardless of how 'perfect' you try to be, you can't control another's journey, especially our children's.

It's all a part of the journey. But how much easier would that journey be if we could just invite in some self-acceptance, self-love and self-nurturance when we need it the most? How much easier will we move through these inevitable challenges if we surrender to the flow and choose ease and grace over striving for perfection or believing we should be doing better?

What if it was all perfect at this moment, regardless of how challenging it is? How would you feel knowing every single one of these challenges is just a moment in time and necessary for the moments of joy to occur?

Because let's be honest, those moments of joy, like a baby's first smile, the first time they hug you cuddled up on the couch relaxing with a movie. The excitement on their face at Christmas or simply the words 'I love you, Mum,' is all we need to completely dissolve and forget the hard days.

Ash Moreland
You Matter Too

Being a mother is so easy until you have kids! At least it was for me. I judgementally watched mothers and their children, commentating in my head. I had grand ideas about what I would and wouldn't do, even more so, what my kids would and wouldn't do when I became a mother. I now laugh at the expense of my naïve younger self.

Since becoming a mother at twenty-three and raising a son with multiple diagnoses prone to dysregulation, plus having a daughter who is a living, breathing clone of myself, I've struggled with all the opinions. All the self-judgement and self-doubt, the mistakes, guilt, criticism, and the unrelenting drive to protect my babes and defend them at any cost gave me many fears and subsequent beliefs that impacted me and my relationship with my kids, myself, and others.

I quickly learned that I was not the mother to my kids that I wanted to be or that they needed me to be, and I commenced my own healing journey. From my own experience and the wisdom I've acquired over years of working with many other women, some fundamental messages constantly arise when navigating motherhood. It is an honour to share these here.

Self-care is more than...

Pampering yourself and surface-level pep-ups are fantastic. Do you love getting your hair done? You go, girl! Enjoy a pedicure? Yes! Massage? Oh, boy, take my money.

But these surface-level pep-ups won't cut it if you're in a chronic state of stress.

Navigating returning to work or maintaining a home or both, plus sleep deprivation, unmet needs, lack of support, and being needed day and night, can add to the stress. Our nervous system isn't designed to be activated with so many demands and so little restoration for such long periods. When this happens, the self-care quickly turns into self-soothing or self-preserving, and the behaviours that result indicate our primal stress responses, fight, flight or freeze.

Fight mode mum might be reactive, snappy and yelling a lot. Flight mode mum, my flavour of a stress response, copes by trying to control things or distract themselves from the stressors. She rushes, always keeps busy, micromanages, and overthinks. Freeze mode mum manages by dissociating or numbing. They might spend hours upon hours scrolling social media, binge-watching television, or isolating themselves in any way they can.

Aside from these inherent behaviours, sleep is likely hindered, and appetite is likely impacted by craving unhealthy foods, insatiable hunger or lack of appetite. You'll find your sex drive on one end of the extreme, either non-existent or ravenous. If you relate to any of this, fluffy self-care is like using a bandaid to reattach an amputated leg. Genuine self-care looks like setting boundaries, saying no to things that don't sit well in your spirit, having courageous conversations, asking for help, and prioritising your needs over those of others, which leads me to the next point.

Your needs matter

Human infants depend on their mother or another for survival for the most prolonged duration of any other animal. When we have little people who literally *need* us to survive, and we often navigate that motherhood journey somewhat unsupported, it is very easy to disconnect from our own needs. When we habitually abandon our needs for the sake of our children or others for long enough, we eventually reach a point where we don't even know our needs or how to meet them in healthy ways.

While we Mums are superheroes with our ability to wear many hats and juggle every aspect of life, we're still human. Every human has essential needs, some are for survival, like food and shelter. Beyond that, we have emotional and relational needs necessary for healthy neural and mental development and well-being, like certainty, variety, significance, connection, contribution and growth.

If we are so focused on everyone else's needs that we abandon our own, every aspect of our physical, emotional, social, intellectual and spiritual well-being suffers. We hear on aeroplanes, 'fit your own mask first, before fitting others'. There's a paradoxical relationship where to be the best mum, partner, daughter, sister, colleague, friend or anything else that we can be, we burn ourselves out, making it impossible to do any of those things well. Yet, when we prioritise our well-being and are fulfilled, inspired and experiencing joy, we are automatically better equipped to be the mum, partner and all the other things we desire. But what *do* we desire to be? Is it a *good mum*?

Don't buy into the 'good mum' myth

We can invest so much time and effort in being a 'good mum'. We can read parenting books, follow doctors' advice, buy stylish clothes, create a fancy nursery, and cook homemade meals. We can bust our guts to breastfeed, buy our kids treats, and sacrifice or work hard to provide everything we possibly can for them. The problem is, we invest all this time, effort, energy and money into being or doing the things that society values and suggests make us a 'good mum', but is that really the answer?

Sadly, there is no amount of stylish clothes, abundant bank balances or breast milk that will make it easy for a child to share their favourite toy, prevent tantrums in public, or ensure that the teen years are smooth sailing. So, what's the key to emotional and behavioural regulation and developing a healthy, safe, loving relationship with our children?

Let's start by asking these questions

Can I be present enough with my dysregulated child, often the 'naughty' or 'misbehaving' child, to co-regulate, bringing them back to emotional safety?

Can I remain regulated enough to connect with them in their moment of need more deeply and respond from a place of love and compassion?

Could I remain sovereign to the judgements and criticisms of others to prioritise and validate my child's emotional expression at that moment?

Can I set healthy boundaries that are in my child's best interest, even if it means they're unhappy with it?

To be honest, for the first eight years of my motherhood journey, the answer to these questions was no for me. According to the world's values, I was a 'good mum', but when my children's emotions or behaviours escalated, I'd spiral into guilt and shame. As a result, I'd completely dissociate or experience severe anxiety and want to punish my kids or use fear to suppress their behavioural or emotional outbursts.

That was all I knew, and my nervous system's innate and natural drive was wired towards feeling unsafe if my kids were 'out of control' and reacting from a survival instinct in those moments. If you relate to this, find it in your heart to have loving self-compassion because, like every other human on the planet and me, you're doing the best you can with the resources you have. But, even if our best isn't too crash hot, no one can expect us to do better because we can't do better than our best at any given moment. So, the good news is, if you've identified that you do want to do better, we can, but we have to be willing to step into change.

Navigating Motherhood

We have the power to choose change

The only time we ever have is right now. We can not go back and change the past, and we will also never get this time back, so we are constantly faced with a choice as to how we spend every 'now' moment. Our relationships, financial position, health status and life, in general, are all the culmination of every choice made in our past moments, whether we made them consciously or not.

Take a moment to reflect on each aspect of your life. Are you exactly where you want to be and fully satisfied? If not, that's okay! However, if you change nothing, what will each of these aspects of your life be like six months from now? A year from now? Five years from now? If that doesn't sound very appealing, you now have the leverage you need to *want* to make a change.

Although we can't change our past, we can learn from it. We can change our priorities and intentions and create a different future that more closely reflects the life we want. If you know you want to make a change but don't know how, many practitioners, coaches, mentors and therapists globally can support you on this journey of empowered change.

It's the greatest investment we could ever make for ourselves, our kids, and our future.

Gary Keller says in his book, *The One Thing*, 'Your present now and all future now's are undeniably determined by the priority you live in the moment'. So, upon realising my thoughts, actions and behaviours as a mother weren't aligned with what I desired, nor what I wanted for my kid's future, I was faced with a decision to change. That started with a conscious look at my priorities.

Priorities are essential but must be adaptive

As a mother, I desire safe and deep connections with my children, resulting in a beautiful, loving relationship. Once I established this desire, I could prioritise things in each new now that presented itself so that each passing now became another step in the direction of my desired outcomes. For example, getting caught up in dirty dishes, washing, cooking, working, and other day-to-day life necessities was easy. However, if my child was seeking connection and I was prioritising doing the dishes, the 'cost' of doing the dishes was very expensive—the price was connection with my child.

This priority doesn't align with my desire for a safe and deep connection with my kids. So, continuing to prioritise in this way wouldn't result in healthy relationships in the future. Yet, if my child was happily entertained and their needs met, the cost of doing the dishes at that moment was very low with no connection expense.

Sometimes things *are* essential and need to be done at that very moment. In this case, communicating this priority without compromising connection is critical. It might be something like, 'I hear you, sweetheart, and it is really important to me that I can give you all of my attention. I really need to do this task right now. But as soon as I'm done with that, I'll be able to do what you need. Would that be okay?'

This meets their need for significance by acknowledging that you see and hear them and that they are important to you. It meets their need for certainty by being clear on what you're doing and why. It also tells them when they can expect to have your attention. It asks permission, which invites them to give further information about the intensity of their priority. This subsequently invites you to reassess the priority cost at that moment.

But what if we get it wrong?

It's okay to make mistakes

Always remember that you are *exactly* the mum your children need, and they're *exactly* the children you need because you chose one another in this lifetime. If you've reflected and identified that you haven't been the mum you want to be, or you've made mistakes in the past, acknowledge that it was the best you could have done with the emotional, energetic, and physical resources available to you.

There is no such thing as failure, only winning or learning. Being compassionate towards ourselves for our past, or even present, mistakes and being vulnerable and transparent with our children about our imperfections is one of the greatest gifts our kids can receive. Imagine growing up learning that it's safe to make mistakes and that we can learn from them and grow. All humans are imperfect, and even in our imperfections, we're still worthy of love.

Mistakes are like a lighthouse. They guide us towards a better path. Since our future hasn't happened yet, we can implement the learnings from our past mistakes to create the future we want to have, to be the mum we want to be. Ultimately, we can accept things as they are and strive to do better. But what if it's too late?

It's never too late

The perfect time to make a positive change is now. Even if you're in a difficult phase, or your children are older, and you feel 'the damage is done', it is never too late to bring safety, love and connection back into a relationship. If we dare to dive deep into our own healing and growth, it shows kids that we can change, do better and have gratitude for our past experiences, and they can too. Their past does not define them.

Final remarks

This whole 'Mum' gig is no joke. Yet, despite the bleeding nipples, relentless sleep deprivation, tantrums, social dramas, playing taxi, and all the other developmentally normal challenges that arise at each stage of life, we couldn't love our little humans more if we tried.

When we can really embody the learnings and wisdom within this book and learn to be present and fully receptive to the needs of ourselves and our kids, meeting them becomes infinitely more accessible, and this journey is an enjoyable journey worth taking. Our kids will not remember how close and connected they felt to us by the things we were doing or buying *for* them, but in how we were *with* them—present, kind, patient, accepting, gentle and loving. Finally, they learn to be those things to themselves by observing us being them to ourselves, too. So love your 'self' well—you're worth it.

Ash Moreland

Hi, I'm Dr Ashleigh Moreland! I'm a highly energetic and passionate neuroscientist, best-selling author, speaker, lecturer, therapist and consultant on a mission to impact the masses. I grew up in a small country town in Queensland, Australia, and moved solo to Melbourne at sixteen to pursue my academic career.

With a heavy academic focus since 2007, I subsequently completed my PhD in neuroplasticity and built a highly successful career, recognised for excellence across teaching, research and leadership. Whilst still research active and primarily supervising PhD candidates, my focus and passion have shifted to helping people on a large scale to overcome barriers to being present and connecting with themselves and others through awareness, education and trauma-informed transformation.

This passion became a serious and urgent quest for me after having my first child in 2013 following a severely traumatic birth experience. My child went on to develop significant emotional, mental and neuro-developmental challenges. After being dissatisfied with the opinions of various medical experts, I put my academic skill set to good use and became hyper focused on learning everything possible about healing from a holistic mind-body-spirit perspective.

Becoming a single mother of two following four pregnancy losses and the dissolution of my marriage in 2018, I was forced to dive even more deeply into extreme ownership, self-responsibility, and personal and relational healing. These experiences and significant further study and practitioner training armed me with expertise on psychological, biological and neurological drivers of behavioural and relational experiences in children and adults alike and tools to change them.

Now remarried and surrounded by fulfilling and nurturing relationships, my kids are happy and healthy. My life is enriched by using my knowledge, skill sets, and lived experience to impact individuals, couples, families and workplaces worldwide. I partner with people to transform their relationships with themselves and others, enhance performance and productivity, and achieve deep connection and presence through nervous system integration and regulation.

You can learn more or request a booking to work with me at:
Website: www.drashleighmoreland.com
Tik Tok: www.tiktok.com/@dr.ashleighmoreland?lang=en
Facebook: www.facebook.com/dr.ashleighmoreland or
www.facebook.com/BigPeopleLittlePeopleAU
Instagram: www.instagram.com/dr.ashleighmoreland/

Aimee Brown
Making Health Simple

'It is health that is the real wealth, and not pieces of gold and silver.'
– Mahatma Gandhi

I'm a mum of three, wife, business owner, holistic chiropractor, and personal trainer, and I run ultra marathons. Phew, so it is safe to say that I'm pretty busy. Life is full. It is also safe to say that I must be functioning at my best to do all of these things and do them well. I need to take care of myself so that I can take care of my kids, family and friends, as well as take care of my clients, run a business and run ultra marathons.

I know you may be sitting there reading this, thinking that we all know we should be taking care of ourselves and our health. We've all heard the saying on aeroplanes, 'Put the oxygen masks on to save yourself first as you can't help someone else if you aren't alive'. But so many mums find it hard and complicated to do. We constantly read and consume media suggesting that being healthy is complicated and rigid. Either that or it is offering the next magic pill. It is so hard to scroll through social media without seeing it, isn't it? Juice cleanses and 28-day challenges, a tablet for this or that, exercise plans to promise the world, promises of a supermodel body and yogi mindset.

But what is the chance of most of us doing and achieving all these strict and complicated things? Minimal, right? Especially without having to stop living your life and doing the important day-to-day things, like looking after your child, trying to function on limited sleep and keeping on top of that never-ending mental to-do list.

So, then it all gets thrown into the too-hard basket. Being healthy and well becomes another ball to juggle, something else on your to-do list. Another thing on your already overloaded plate. You feel like a failure because you can't do it all. You start things and give up. You can't balance it all or fit it all in. This then results in your mental and physical health suffering.

Let's be clear, having a baby is amazing! But it can also be hugely stressful, and we want to decrease your stress, not add to it. I've been there, and I am still there. My kids are six, eight and ten. They take up even more time now with all their activities, so it's as if I have even less time for myself and my health.

As a holistic chiropractor, I care for pre and postpartum women and for babies, kids and families. I see the impact having or trying to have children has on women, physically and emotionally, no matter the age of the children or how many they have. Most people recognise physical stresses. We know that growing and birthing a human takes a toll on us.

Our bodies are designed for it, but it still impacts us. Huge hormonal shifts combined with a lack of sleep, holding, carrying, and feeding your baby can make you sit and stand in weird postures and positions. Think it will get easier as the children get older? Sorry to tell you, but it doesn't.

Then the emotional stress takes just as much of a toll on us. You're trying to work out what to do and how to keep this little human alive, at the same time as you are sleep deprived and hormonal. Hello Stress. You search online for all sorts of random things at 3am, and mentally you are exhausted from trying to work it all out. Advice is coming at you from all angles, and you don't know who or what to listen to. Then, just as you think you have it worked out, you read something that contradicts what you have decided, and you get sent into another head spin and emotional spiral. You feel so alone. You worry you are doing it all wrong. Sound familiar? I know it does to me.

At this point, you know you need to drink more water and less coffee, exercise and eat nutritious food, not chocolate, but that just all seems way too hard. I know. I've been there.

I've done the juice cleanses and the fasting. I've done the Paleo and Keto. I've done yoga, Pilates, high-intensity gym workouts, running, and swimming. I've done meditation and breathing. I've done at-home workouts and paid for expensive gym memberships. I've had meals and meal kits delivered. I've even given up coffee.

I've tried it all, and it honestly was all so stressful. It seemed way too hard. It increased my stress levels instead of decreasing them. So, I'd look for the next thing. The next diet or routine that promised me the world, everything from energy and abs. And the thing is, I never found that magic pill. Even if it did deliver what it promised, it would never be sustainable long-term.

But I finally found what works. And it not only works for me but also for many women I've worked with. And that is to keep it simple. Do the simple things regularly. That will add up and make significant changes to your health and mindset.

It's all about creating simple healthy habits that become part of your day and allow you to live your life and enjoy it. So health becomes part of your life, instead of changing your whole life to fit in the new routine or diet. Health should be simple and easy, not rigid and restrictive.

Start with simple. Find one thing from the lists below that you can focus on to create a new habit. One that you think is easy for you to fit in right now and commit to every day. Then when you have one solidly happening, come back to this chapter and pick the next thing you can work on to create the next healthy habit.

Let's start with movement

Want to exercise more? Amazing! But don't start with doing hours a week. As it's likely not going to last if you try that. So start small. Do it consistently. And it's more likely to become a habit that you can sustain.

- Try to start solo with ten minutes a week, no partner and no children. It can make a world of difference to you mentally and physically, then build from there.
- Do a few squats while holding your child and walking up and down the hallway. Do some push-ups.
- Commit to doing five-to-ten minutes of stretching a day. Split it up into one-to-two-minute slots of time if you need to.
- Go to one class per week and then add a few walks.

Sounds almost too simple right? It's about building slowly and steadily. That makes it sustainable. By building slowly, you are more likely to do it. If the above sounds easy, being more ambitious is also okay.

Set yourself a goal like a five kilometer fun run or a marathon, even an ultramarathon. Doing something like that, having big goals, is okay. It's okay to be an ambitious mum. Your kids will love it when they grow up.

Most importantly, find a way to move your body that feels good to you. For me, it's running further than most people like to drive. I also didn't start doing this until my kids were a little older, not newborn babies. If running isn't for you, it may be swimming, hiking, weightlifting, or yoga. Find what you love and do that. It will make it much easier to get motivated. It's really important, though, to get checked after birth with a women's health physio. They will let you know what exercise you can do safely.

Now let's talk food

When it comes to diets, let's just say that I think most people don't actually need one. When did the focus move to juice cleanses, Keto, Paleo or shakes and get away from just eating real food? Fresh fruit and produce and lots of plant-based foods. And no, that doesn't mean you can't eat meat. It just means you need to eat a lot of fruit and vegetables because most people don't eat enough. I also know it's easy to get distracted keeping another human, or three or more alive, and you can forget to eat.

So that's when it is important to do some simple things to have healthy food ready.

- As much as possible, stay away from pre-packaged foods. If you grab pre-packaged, grab it from the fruit and vegetable section. There are some great options. Yes, this will mean you need to pre-plan and prepare meals, but it makes it much easier in the long run. Those days when the kids are crazy, you are tired and can't even stop to breathe or put the kids down. We all have them, and they are easier if healthy food is ready. Also, if it's one day of takeaway, that's okay.
- Also, accept food offered to you by family or friends. If someone offers home-cooked meals, always say yes.
- Have snacks like cut-up fruit and vegetables, nuts, boiled eggs, and protein balls. This will make it easier to grab and go healthy options.
- Don't be afraid of protein, good fats and carbs. Your body needs them all in balance. As a female, it is important to ensure you get enough protein for many things, including hormone health, muscle growth, general health and weight loss. Following that, please know don't exclude any food groups unless you medically have to.
- Kids and adults love pick plates—things you have in the fridge cut up and put on a plate. They love it, and we love it because it's quick, easy and healthy.

Let's talk hydration

How much water do you drink? And no, water in coffee doesn't count. In my experience, people overestimate how much water they drink daily. This means that most people don't get enough in. For the typical woman, it's recommended that she drinks at least two litres a day.

Does that sound like a lot? Wonder how you can do that?

- Have a glass by your bed and make yourself drink it before you leave the bedroom in the morning.
- Drink a bottle on the way to work.
- Every time you walk into the kitchen, have a glass of water.
- Don't like the taste? Add some fruit to flavour it.
- Have herbal tea. If caffeine free, it counts to your water intake.
- Instead of five coffees, replace one cup of coffee with a cup of water.
- Don't start with an extra litre in a day if you find it hard. Just add an extra cup to start with.

Time to talk sleep

Sleep is often the hardest thing for a new mum or any mum. It is often interrupted, disrupted, or you stay up later than you know you should just to get some alone time. We've all been there and know that we need to get more sleep. Sleep deprivation is a form of torture for a reason. It takes a massive toll physically and mentally on your body.

Tips to create healthy habits around sleep

- Sleep in a dark room and make it light as soon as you are awake for the day. It helps the hormones that regular sleep.
- Do some breathing when you get to bed to help your body relax.

- Use guided meditation.
- Take some time to stretch before you get into bed.
- Get off screens at least an hour before bed. This is a hard one, I know.
- Keep a pen and paper by your bed and write down any thoughts you can't get out of your head.
- Get up at the same time each day and go to bed at the same time each night.
- Struggle to get to bed early? Start by trying to go to bed fifteen minutes earlier. Then fifteen minutes earlier than that.

Breathing and grounding

I am sitting here with my feet in the sand, watching whales as I write this. It is incredibly grounding, calming, and great for resetting my nervous system, mind, and body. I know that it is not always possible to be in a remote location and completely switch off. However, there are simple things you can do in your everyday life that will positively impact your health, especially if you do them regularly and consistently. You also don't need to be meditating for hours a week.

Simple habits to introduce into your day

- Close your eyes, stop and take some deep breaths. Set your timer on your phone for two minutes, then go for three minutes until you get up to fifteen minutes. Sleep-deep breathing helps get your body out of stress mode and relax.
- Get barefoot in nature. The grass or the beach works well. Go to your local park if you don't have grass at home.
- Find any time in the day to take a few deep breaths. Even doing a few in the car or the shower is better than nothing.

- Can't get outside? Splash some water on your face, play some music you love and smile. It is all about changing your state. Simple things can make a massive difference to your mindset.

Forming new healthy habits can seem like a huge mountain to climb, but know that it is just one step at a time. Do one thing that will get you closer to where you want to be with your health. One small thing will start you moving in the right direction. Start small, focus on one habit, and then build on it each week. It's also okay if things don't go to plan some days. That's motherhood, right? But here is the deal, get rid of any guilt surrounding that.

In my opinion, guilt will cause you more issues most of the time than having a bad day and skipping a workout or eating takeaway. The next day is a new day, and the next week is a new week. Stop, breathe, splash some water on your face, turn up the music and dance. Know that you aren't alone. I have been there, and if you feel alone, please reach out to me.

Just remember that it's consistency that counts. It's doing small, simple things, every day or often, not one big thing once. Building slowly and consistently will have the most lasting impact on your health. Remember, you are an individual, and everybody is different. So all this advice is general and from my personal experience. It doesn't replace any individualised health advice from your health care practitioners. Please seek someone who can work with you to reach your health goals.

'Simple things, done consistently, become significant.' - Dr Aimee Brown

Love the idea of keeping health simple? Want to work with me?

I currently see clients at my holistic chiropractic clinic Bespoke Chiropractic Manning. I also have online programs and modules for those people who can't get into the clinic to see me. Going with these modules,

I also have Weekly Wellness for You Cards—A pack of cards designed to give you a simple health focus point for each week. One thing to focus on or find time for, it's that simple. The cards cover all aspects of health, whether it's physical, emotional, or nutritional health. Because we all know the things, we should be doing but need reminding from time to time.

Aimee Brown

Dr Aimee Brown (DC) is a Holistic Chiropractor, personal trainer, ultra marathon runner and mother of three based in Manning, Perth. Aimee is passionate about the mind and body connection. She takes a multidisciplinary approach to treatment, looking at all aspects of well-being from nervous system health, stress management and lifestyle to mindset, sleep and exercise.

With her mission to help clients achieve optimal health and well-being, Aimee recognises the interconnected nature of physical and emotional health. No issue is addressed in isolation.

As well as chiropractic treatment, Aimee offers online programs and weekly wellness cards.

A strong believer that the biggest changes to our health start with small steps, Aimee provides guidance and support to help people regain control of their well-being, one inch at a time. Aimee's ultimate goal is to help people achieve optimal health, integrating the mind and body connection so that we can all live our life to the fullest.

When Aimee's not with clients, crafting affirmation cards or partaking in ultra marathons, you'll likely find her spending time with her loving husband and beautiful children, camping or getting lost in a book.

Instagram www.instagram.com/draimeebrown
Facebook www.facebook.com/draimeebrownchiro
www.draimeebrown.com

Marilou Coombe
Navigating The Journey

Before having children, I was the baby whisperer. You know, the ones who hold crying babies, and the baby stops crying—the ones who have no issues with toddler tantrums. I loved babysitting gigs as a teen and later being an au pair to three young children under four at the tender age of twenty-four in the USA. But that didn't prepare me for having my own children.

Getting pregnant was such a journey. We were about to see a specialist when a miracle occurred, and it finally happened. From pregnancy to becoming a first-time mother, I was so focused on the birth and excited about being pregnant that I didn't overthink beyond that. But then again, how could I predict all the challenges I would face?

The pregnancy itself was a roller-coaster.

We almost lost the baby at nine weeks. I was on bed rest for several weeks and took it easy for the remainder of the pregnancy. Then I went into four-day labour, six weeks early. All the certainty of what I'd be like as a mother went right out the window, especially after a nurse came in and told me not to hold the baby for too long as he needed his sleep to grow. My OCD kicked in, which then turned into anxiety.

There was so much shame and guilt during the first six months of parenting. I couldn't breastfeed as I thought. I couldn't settle my baby as I did with other babies. I was heightened and exhausted simultaneously. I had so many *shoulds* in my life, and I felt like I failed miserably at meeting my own self-imposed expectations. The baby didn't sleep like I thought he should. He didn't stop crying as he should. He didn't go by the textbooks as he should.

A pivotal moment in my life as a mother happened when my baby was six months old. One morning, I finished dressing him on my bed, and as I picked him up, I lost control of the muscles in my arm and dropped him. Thankfully, the bed caught him. However, I was mortified, and mentally I spiralled fast. I felt like I couldn't take care of this beautiful little soul. Why did he choose me as his mother? I did not feel like I deserved him. This had a huge impact on our family life and the upcoming changes we found out we needed to implement.

After a trip to the doctor and a specialist who ordered blood tests, they confirmed that I had coeliac disease. The sadness and relief that overcame me were indescribable. Sadness and anxiety over what I could and couldn't eat. Relief that I had an answer to the many doubts over my body being able to give birth to this baby and care for him. I simply wasn't receiving the nutrients to function well, let alone support him. I had a choice to let this condition beat me or rise above it to be the best mother I could be. I was able to look for solutions.

Little did I know at the time that was the beginning of my journey to healing and self-development. As I found solutions, gratitude started to replace the frustration and anxiety I felt. I began to learn more about clean eating after making the mistake of eating all the gluten-free packaged foods and, for the first time in my life, started stacking on the weight. I learnt about how my body worked and what it needed. I started to learn what it really meant to have self-love, self-care, and self-nurture. Eating fewer packaged foods and more whole foods with no fillers meant that the best part was when the baby started solids, he was on a healthy start to life.

I learned about all the numbers and colours that lace our foods and affect our health. So many events throughout my life began to make sense. Insomnia and what I thought was bulimia from the age of sixteen, depression and other ailments all had light shed on them. My body was simply saying no to something I was ingesting that it didn't accept.

We easily fell pregnant with our second child a year later. In fact, it was magical. My body allowed me to feel the process of impregnation. But the excitement didn't last long. At ten weeks, I started bleeding and feared I'd lost the baby. All the old fears and anxiety came back. The mistrust in my body and the *shoulds* reared their ugly heads. We headed for an ultrasound, and the sonographer confirmed there were two sacs. We lost one baby, but the other survived and had a healthy heartbeat.

For three weeks, I bled the miscarriage naturally—more bed rest and slowing down. When we thought we could announce the pregnancy at thirteen weeks, we were told we were at high risk for a chromosomal abnormality and that we could 'see what happens' or have further tests to confirm. It was a terrible time to learn that their dad and I have different opinions on those types of decisions. So we held our breaths and didn't mention it to anyone. And despite it all being okay in the end, no one knew about the baby except those we had face-to-face interactions with until he came earthside.

In the middle of a house renovation and three weeks early, I started having contractions in what used to be our dining room. I think I scared the builders with my screams. As we made our way to the birthing suites, I tapped into my inner strength and knowledge of my body's ability to birth. I learned a lot about hypnobirthing and using essential oils to support me. After seven hours, a beautiful, healthy boy was born who latched on and breastfed naturally. It was a magical and surreal experience; beautiful healing took place at that moment. My brain and body were receiving evidence of what could occur when we trusted and surrendered.

It was amusing and empowering how I could stand in my power with my second. No one bothered me in the hospital. Nobody told me what to do. Even when a nurse came in and I was co-sleeping, she let us be. No one was grabbing my breasts and trying to feed this baby. No one told me not to spoil or hold him for too long. It was the start of trusting my intuition as a mother and following my child's lead.

It was so wonderful seeing my eldest interact with his sibling. It was love at first sight. It was such a blessing how he wanted to be with his baby. They fed at the same time. We all napped together. It was such a different experience and journey than my first time around. But then again, I was more of a relaxed mother. I was different. So, of course, the experience was different.

As the boys grew, they did so much together and for each other. My youngest only ate solids at six months when his brother fed him. They cuddled and loved each other. We had play dates at the park, beach and in our backyard. It was beautiful and yet, at times, lonely.

In my own experience, I'm convinced our firstborns are here to pave the way, clear the hurts and limiting beliefs, and teach us our growth abilities. While our subsequent births are to heal and grow us beyond what we thought we originally needed. Our children, in fact, forever, will trigger us and gift us the opportunities to heal.

So, despite this love nest we created, I was lonely and felt unfulfilled as a person beyond motherhood. I've always wanted to be a mum, so why wasn't I happy just being a mum? Something I couldn't quite put my finger on was missing, and I felt like I was just passing the days not being fully present.

As everything happens for us in divine timing, a friend gifted me a ticket to a four-day personal development seminar held interstate. So naturally, all sorts of mind monsters came to play. I am not worthy. I can't be away from the boys. I can't afford the flights and accommodation. All the excuses! Luckily, with the help of their dad and this friend, I was able to get away and experience the most life-changing event, which helped me realign with my values and who I truly am.

This gave me the boost and focus on becoming a better mother and role model to these amazing young souls who did choose me as their mum in this lifetime. They really were my driving force, and I finally understood the purpose of doing something bigger than just for myself. I don't believe I could raise young, strong, compassionate men if I weren't walking the talk.

I then started working part-time online to support others in navigating their parenting journey. What a gift my experiences have been! Despite having a degree in Psychology, nothing taught me like the real-life experiences I've been able to reflect on to help others.

This led me to delve into human behaviour and our responses to it, especially children's behaviour. I went on to obtain training in life coaching, NLP, Access Consciousness, mental health support and kids yoga. I have created my own business and online presence to support families to thrive and be aligned with their values to be the best they can be.

I love what I do and encourage my boys daily to do what they love. Through my role modelling, they are becoming their own little entrepreneurs, and in COVID-19 lockdowns, my youngest held online yoga classes for young yogis. His sessions were a success, and at seven years old, he made A$70 for twenty minutes of an online presence. The things learned from that experience were priceless and boosted his confidence for life.

This all led to following their lead recently and leaving the school system. It is a whole new pathway to navigate. Initially, I took it on as my job to make them happy. Then quickly realised that is a sure formula for my own personal misery.

We are now co-creating and walking this path together to what it all means to us. Learning occurs at all times, and it needs to be fun. We rarely get it perfect, but then we learnt there is no such thing as perfect. It is all about being open, growing and curious. It is about doing life!

To be honest, there are moments now where I wish I could go back and do those younger years differently, but then I remind myself they are still young enough. It's never too late to be doing things the way we want. It's all about being present and in the moment. Spending time in the past leads to depression, and living in the future leads to anxiety. I have experienced both states of mind, and I chose the now! It's a daily practice!

Lessons and revelations

- The extent of my own inner strength.
- How to live fully aligned with my values.
- How to follow my own inner compass.
- How to really take radical responsibility and care for myself, including my physical and mental.
- How to drop the should and need to be perfect.
- How to stop being a people pleaser.
- That our children are a reflection of us, they will always mirror us, what needs healing, where we shine, and what needs changing.
- Regardless of the challenges, if our mindset is strong and aligned with our spirit, magik still occurs, and we can achieve anything.
- That respectful communication and treating our children the way we want to be treated trumps being right.
- That my connection to my family is more important than doing dishes, cleaning or anything else, especially when they need me to be there for them.
- I must be my best to raise these boys to be their best.
- That growth and learning are ongoing processes.
- That small babies have small problems and big babies have big problems. Appreciate and deal with the now!

- I'm the expert on my children's and my family's needs.
- Conflict is present when my reality doesn't meet my expectations.
- As Ralph Waldo Emmerson says, 'It's not the destination, it's the journey.'

We all know that parenting and motherhood don't come with a manual. In fact, the reality is that for each child, we create their own manual.

What a journey it's been, and no doubt will continue to be. And this is why my business is all about helping families thrive, helping parents be the best role models for their children, and supporting youth to shine their light into the world. Using my own journey to mentor others and my training in the field of human behaviour has helped many navigate parenthood. I now offer the support I wish I had when I first became a mother.

Once we sign up for the parenting contract, it is for life! I'm so in awe of the young men my boys are becoming and the person I'm growing to be in that process. And amongst this journey, I get to witness and help others do the same for their family.

So much gratitude and joy fill my heart as I navigate the journey of motherhood.

Marilou Coombe

I'm Marilou Coombe, a passionate coach, mentor, author, yoga teacher, workshop facilitator, retreat planner and youth worker. I'm also a Mumma to two energetic young boys who inspire me to be a better version of myself daily.

When I became a mother in my early thirties, I thought I was prepared and could handle everything. However, my degree in Psychology and various other certificates, as grand as they were, had no instructions on how to be the mum my firstborn needed. So I had to start from scratch like all new mums and look closely at what mattered to me most in life. I delved into my values, beliefs, mindset, and ancestral trauma and studied various subjects that collectively dealt with the mind, body and soul.

At that point, I realised that working with families and empowering children made me the happiest and was where I could add the most value back to society. I wanted to pass the knowledge to other families on how to help their children thrive the best way they can! And I knew then that to teach my children to walk their talk, I had to lead by example and be aware of how I showed up in life!

Marilou Coombe

I made it my absolute mission to empower children, in particular, to have a strong self-belief that stemmed from their core to achieve anything they set out to do. That's why I created a space to achieve my goal of empowering families and children to connect and be their best possible selves!

You can connect with me on the following channels:
FB: www.facebook.com/orchestratewithmarilou
Web: orchestratewithmarilou.newzenler.com
Email: marilou@orchestrate.cc

Diana Welch
Expectations Versus Reality

'If we find ourselves emotionally upset or disappointed – an unchecked expectation has slipped through the gate.' – Diana Welch

Chinese women have a tradition where they're not allowed to place their feet on the ground for four weeks after they give birth. Of course, going to the toilet is allowed, but the goal is to replenish her energy, blood, sense of self as a woman and her new role as a mother. This time is also for the mother to be and feel fully supported by her family. The older women of the family come together to cook nourishing meals, clean, and tend to the other children, if there are any. This allows the new mother to rest, recover and connect with her new baby, learning the cues and understanding what bub is trying to tell her with their cries. The Chinese believe this time is sacred. Allowing the woman to recuperate during the four weeks helps her recover emotionally and physically. They call the tradition 'sitting the month'.

Even in the Western world, we understand that we can't recover this time once it has gone. In Western cultures, there's a need to push to do it all. This is the masculine side of ourselves. We don't allow ourselves to be supported in many ways because we don't want anything to mar the thought of us being strong independent women. As new mothers, a really important goal is allowing ourselves to slow down and be supported, not only during the first months of our new baby's life but also as a mother who feels overwhelmed and fatigued.

Motherhood is a gift that not all of us get to have, and when we're too frazzled, stressed, overworked and overwhelmed, we lose that understanding. Finding balance between the Masculine and Feminine energies we all have is a fabulous way to start to get to know ourselves and ourselves as a mother.

Divine Feminine energy is intuitive (this is why we have 'mother's intuition'), receptive and open, flowing with ease, nurturing and tender, sensitive and emotional.

Divine Masculine energy allows us to have discipline and be organised logical and assertive, independent by showing we don't need support, practical, strong and capable.

We've transitioned into the masculine world. Working longer hours for yourself or an employer means children are in daycare longer. Ensuring your home looks put together and tidy, eating healthy, exercising, being a wife, mother and lover and continuously pushing and striving for the next goal. We want to be better than yesterday. I find that masculine energy is where we see where many of our expectations of others and ourselves lie.

Society today has driven home the masculine need for success and winning, pushing our expectations to be better and greater. However, we all have different ideas of what success actually is. Continually striving for that tick of approval, whether from external validation from others or what we believe we want, keeps us stuck in a loop of expectations that can lead to possible emotional upset and disappointments.

Current masculine practice within our society pushes mothers to think they must be up and shopping within days of giving birth. I have seen quite a few of my patients out at the local shopping centre, pushing a new pram and a new baby around with their partner and shopping for the baby, sometimes within days of giving birth. This type of expectation is very masculine and drains our energy, which hasn't replenished from giving birth. It shows similar characteristics to the *Lion King*, where new parents are like Mufasa showing Simba or their new cub to the world and the Pride Lands.

Though what is suffering in this masculine society is our own divine feminine. Our divine feminine needs us to slow down, rest, recover and hold our babies close, giving them love, compassion and understanding. And, in turn, giving ourselves that love, compassion and understanding that we so desperately crave when our life situations are changed. Our feminine needs to be supported. It needs to feel that support from ourselves and our families and friends.

Our divine feminine is screaming for support, collaboration, kindness and love. *Self-love. Self-compassion. Self-kindness.* And learning what our babies are trying to tell us from the beginning.

People say, 'It takes a village to raise a child,' and I still believe it's as true and correct today as it was more than a century ago. Probably even more so in today's masculine culture. However, it's very rare to have a village around us because we've become so independent and controlled and don't like to ask for help from family or friends.

Deciding when to sit in our masculine energy is needed, and so very important as it becomes a vital role as a parent. When we sit in the masculine side of motherhood, we become rigid, organised, controlled, independent and constantly on the go. We must be organised and practical to ensure the baby bag is packed with everything we may need when we leave the house. Though we also need the masculine side to tell us when we need to ask for support and ensure we are asking the people who can give us that support.

There are definitely times when this is needed, though remembering that we have a feminine side is also really important. It's finding that space in our feminine to nurture and listen to that side as well—the nurturing, passive, patient, balanced, flexible, understanding, kind side, the side with vulnerability. These qualities will help us find our natural mothering style and allow us to hold our new babies with a level of understanding and love.

By looking at our expectations, beliefs and ideals, we can release a lot of what we 'think' society wants from us and come back to standing in our own authenticity. This can lead us to find happiness within ourselves and our family circle, ensuring we are not constantly looking outside ourselves for that validation or happiness.

As new mothers, we find ourselves tired and fatigued a lot. Allowing ourselves to rest when needed can build our energetic reserves and help us cope in hectic times. However, when we are constantly on the go, we find that we continually push, leaving you feeling even more deflated and our energy defeated.

By examining our expectations, we can start to reality-check and build strategies to help communicate our expectations around certain areas in our life, especially motherhood. This will start to show you where you're setting expectations that are outside of your control and show us the patterns of how we're setting these expectations that can lead to ongoing disappointment in our lives.

When we have expectations around something, anything, we can fill ourselves with the possibility of hurt, pain, annoyance and disappointment if it doesn't go to the plan we've created for ourselves in our mind. We don't really feel much or assess when the expectations are positive because we've already moved on to the next goal or challenge in our mind, setting new, mostly unconscious expectations around what we want to have or happen.

We're always setting expectations of others and ourselves in our lives, whether we know it or not and this is done both unconsciously and consciously by building expectations of how we believe things should be. We always want things in our lives to look and be a certain way, and this is what we classify as expectations. We glamorise an event or a person in our mind and then hold them to those expectations we have created. When that doesn't come together, we find ourselves disappointed if they don't meet those expectations or don't do as we think they should.

All of these unexpressed and unchecked expectations really rob us of our own true happiness. However, when we acknowledge our expectations, we can start to put plans in place and communicate them to others, ensuring we work towards a beneficial outcome.

When I had my second daughter, I really found it hard to accept the 'mess' that was my house. Having my second child and owning my own business, I found that I didn't have as much energy or time after the second birth as I did with my first. There were lots of things that I struggled with. I struggled to tidy the house or even just put things away when I had finished with them due to a lack of energy and the lack of replenishing rest I didn't get.

As a real visual person, I found myself in quiet times when I intended to rest, getting increasingly irritable and annoyed that my house looked 'a mess'. I would try and rush around, putting things away and yelling at my husband about his role or 'lack of helping' along the way. However, by the end of the week, I was so resentful of my husband for not helping me around the house and physically exhausted and depleted that the cycle would start the next week again.

I looked at where I was in my motherhood journey, business and life and realised that what I actually needed to do was come to terms and find peace with the expectations I held at the time—that my husband was a mind reader and that I always needed to have a tidy, well put together house. Because if I didn't come to terms with the fact that I just didn't have the support or energy for the perfect home or a mind-reading husband, I'd find myself in a whole different world of hurt and pain that would take more time and energy to heal. By assessing and checking my expectations surrounding my frustration, I could see I was expecting my husband to tidy the house without being asked.

Once I checked my expectations, I realised that I wasn't even communicating with my husband. I was emotionally exhausted as I didn't even know what I wanted him to help me with. However, allowing myself to rest and recover when I could, gave my feminine energy time to replenish and allowed me the space to communicate lovingly, not the screaming accusatory way I was previously. As a result, not only did I rest and rejuvenate, but our relationship also strengthened as I expressed my needs and expectations without getting upset.

Now ignoring or not seeing the mess didn't happen overnight. Even today, seven years later, I still have moments where I run around the house giving belongings to their owners and telling them to, 'Put them away. This doesn't belong here'. However, taking slow steps to realise that something has to give in your life and making it happen by examining the expectations you hold around people will ensure that you're present as a mother for the kids and in your life.

Happiness is something we are all searching for. By releasing our expectations of what masculine society thinks we should have and sinking into our feminine motherly reality, we can learn to become more present, loveable, worthy and enough. And this may just give you the internal happiness you may well be searching for.

Exercise

Next time you find yourself upset with anyone or an event in your life, even yourself, look at what it is you wanted or expected out of that situation. Ask yourself these questions:

- What did I want?
- What did I get?
- Why is this making me upset? Did I have an unrealistic goal around this?
- Why did I want this outcome?

These questions will help you understand where you have laid your expectations around certain situations and people. This is a great exercise, and I do it often because it shows you where certain patterns of creating expectations are within your life.

When we or someone else has not met an expectation, we get disappointed and upset. By examining these expectations, we can also take responsibility for our part in the situation. Like when I was getting frustrated and angry at my husband when he wasn't helping around the house, I also didn't ask him to help. I just 'expected' he would do that. Examining my expectations benefited us as I didn't communicate or ask for his help. I just yelled at him once a week about not putting anything away!

Diana Welch

Diana is a highly intuitive Energetic Healer and coach who's worked with energy for over twenty years. Diana has also studied and worked with Traditional Chinese Medicine, Reiki, Akashic Records, Crystal Healings, Crystal gridwork, and crystals to help her client's self-care and home healing.

Diana is consistently found on 'Sydney's Top 50 Acupuncturists' list year after year. She is an exceptionally experienced doctor of Traditional Chinese Medicine focusing on fertility and pregnancy. She loves helping women of all stages recognise their feelings and giving them strategies to move through life more easily and joyfully. You will often find Diana walking around the clinic with a patient's baby in her arms or pushing the pram so that the mother can get the rest she needs in the clinic.

Her teachings are based on self-awareness, self-trust and listening to our innate body wisdom. By journeying through her own shadow, Diana has found ways to initiate and teach other women to follow their own souls' journey.

Diana's soul journey is to constantly expand her consciousness, work through self-development and continue learning, which she believes is how she can best help her patients and clients.

Diana also has a profound connection to crystals and has incorporated crystal healing into her clinic and online courses. Diana has a free crystal e-book on Instagram and a free guided meditation at www.dianawelch.com

How you and Diana can work together

One-on-one coaching via zoom
In-person at her Acupuncture clinic in Sydney Australia
Appointments for Energy Healing via zoom
Website
www.dianawelch.com
www.reddragonacupuncture.com.au
Insta
@deewelch_intuitivehealer
@red_dragon_alternativ_medicine
Facebook
Diana Welch – Intuitive Healer
Red Dragon Alternative Medicine

Sarah Holroyd Hill
The Rebirth

'Birth isn't just about making babies, it's about making mums too. You are being invited to reinvent yourself because when a baby is born, so is a mother. And I'll let you in on a secret—the birth of a mother can be even more intense than childbirth.' - Julia Jones

Mama, what you are going through is real, the disorientation, confusion, the overwhelming love, the feeling of reclaiming and releasing. Mama, you are being reborn. You have crossed the sacred threshold into motherhood. The woman you once knew is gone. She will never be again.

Parts of her will travel with you, but other parts will never return. You are on a sacred path of rebirth, remembering, and calling yourself home. This rebirth requires gentleness, holding and nourishment. There will be tears and joy, and you will feel confident and confused simultaneously. Please know that is normal. It is the journey we each go on and holds immense power and growth.

My rebirth

When I became a mother, I was one of the first in our group of friends.

Navigating Motherhood

Through my pregnancy, I felt parts of myself falling away. The party girl, the person who wanted to be out and constantly socialising, started to pull inwards. It was now quiet time to commune with my baby, which filled me up.

My husband was not going through the same transition. He still wanted to go out and hold on to the pre-baby freedom and life.

I remember feeling that I should be able to return to my normal life, to the old me, and I'd just slot a baby into it. I remember struggling, judging myself and feeling like the most boring person in the room. I remember being angry with myself, my husband and friends who didn't get the huge shift happening within me.

I had no words to describe this shift. I didn't realise that every part of me was changing. Not just my physical body but my social, emotional and spiritual world had also shifted. I didn't know that this was normal. I didn't know I was going through a rite of passage that would change me forever.

I sought out books and communities that spoke about this feeling deep inside that something immense was happening to me and that it mattered. It took until I was pregnant with my second baby to claim a deep reverence for this experience.

With his pregnancy, I brought more sacredness to the process. I allowed myself to rest, let go of the stories of what I thought I should be doing, and just be with what was unfolding.

After his birth, I kept my bubble small, allowing us time to integrate the rebirth. But still, the call of productivity came back, the need to cope, be okay, to look after everyone to be busy and productive. So I ended up hugely depleted and exhausted. Looking back, I can see how much I pushed myself and how wrecked I was, but at that moment, I thought that was motherhood.

My third pregnancy and birth were so healing.

I now knew about the importance of the postpartum period. I had words for this rebirth I experienced twice. I understood the process of Matrescence, which is the complete transformation of a woman's psychological, social, emotional, physical and spiritual being as she moves through motherhood.

I knew to the core of me that this was a sacred time, that to step into motherhood resourced and thriving, I had to allow myself to be vulnerable. I had to ask for support and truly let it in. I had to let go of the supermum ideal and embrace the messy, teary, heart-filled transition.

So I planned for my rebirth.

I asked friends to hold a mama blessing to honour the woman I was. I asked friends to feed us after my birth. I told everyone not to expect to see our baby or me until we were ready. I entrusted my husband with the role of gatekeeper. He only let people who filled me up and made me feel safe and loved into my space for the first forty days.

I spent weeks in bed, being fed, massaged, nourished and loved. I spent weeks in bed getting to know this new soul who joined our family and the new me emerging. I mourned my role as a mother of two as I stretched into a mother of four.

At the end of the forty days, my birth team held a sacred ceremony to call me home and honour my body and soul for their journey. Afterwards, I was ready to re-emerge gently into the world, knowing that the rebirth was not complete, that I was still fragile, and that I still needed holding but was ready.

Rebirth and postpartum: Key pillars for healing

There is a sacred window of time after birth where a woman has the chance to heal on all levels, integrate her experience and lay the foundations for lifelong health for themselves and their child.

When we are nourished and allowed the space to heal and integrate after birth, we can step into this new role of a mother feeling ready.

The love hormone

Oxytocin is the hormone of love. It is a vital hormone that supports birth, breastfeeding, bonding and healing. This is permission to focus on what makes you feel happy and loved.

Before birth, make a list of small things that bring you joy that you can add to your postpartum care.

- Massage.
- Warm baths.
- Snuggling in bed.
- People who fill you up.

Also, take this as permission not to have things or people in your space that make you feel stressed or unsafe. This is a sacred space for you and your family. You are allowed to choose who enters.

Nourishing and warming food

Focus on foods that are easy to digest, nourishing, warm and bring you joy.

Support

Ask for help with food, washing, older siblings, and cleaning. This is a time for you to be held and nurtured. Allow the support in.

I coach many mothers who feel worried about being a burden and who don't want to make a fuss or be an inconvenience to others. They feel like they have to repay the support and worry about when they will be able to.

Please let this go. How do you feel when you help others? When someone allows me to support them, I also receive such joy in the exchange.

Know that you do not have to pay the favour back, but that when you are resourced and able, you will pay it forward to someone else in need.

Motherhood isn't meant to be done alone, and the sooner in our journey we learn to let support in, the easier motherhood will be.

Allow the tears and be gentle

You are being reborn. Your body has just created and birthed life, and now you are sustaining a baby while you heal and integrate.

Be gentle with yourself. Allow yourself to feel all the emotions.

Many mothers feel that motherhood should always fill them with joy, but motherhood is complex. It's okay if you feel heavier emotions as well. As we let them flow, we release them from our bodies, and our healing continues.

There will be moments where you feel on top of the world and moments where you feel completely overwhelmed. Trust this is all a part of motherhood.

Choose to love yourself through it all.

Honour your rebirth, honour your experience

Acknowledge it, give words to the experience you are having and know that this is real and it is a universal experience of motherhood.

Know that we can bring honouring to ourselves and our rebirth at any stage. I work with many mums who carry grief years on from their early motherhood.

I support them in acknowledging their grief, allowing them to feel it and understand it is real, and then honouring themselves and their role as a mother. I encourage them to celebrate the amazing woman and mother they are.

Making motherhood sacred

I adore ritual. It is a vital part of my evolution in life and motherhood. It can anchor in and make sacred every moment of our lives.

Rituals can be as simple as lighting a candle with gratitude in your heart.

Navigating Motherhood

It can be gathering with friends, sitting in a circle and speaking from your heart.

It can be giving offerings to Mama Earth, connecting with nature and bringing a deep presence to the moment.

My children and I like to light incense and pray thanks to the earth, trees, bugs, birds and all nature as we place it in our garden.

It can be creating space daily to listen to a meditation, have a cup of cacao or connect with your family.

Motherhood is sacred, your journey is sacred, and you matter.

Sarah Holroyd Hill

Sarah is a mum of three, a birth and motherhood coach and a ceremonialist.

She provides holistic education and coaching for birth, postpartum and motherhood. She also offers personalised ceremonies to honour the rites of passage we go through as women and community sound healings and circles.

Sarah supports mothers in remembering their sacredness, intuition, strength, and power as a woman who trusts in herself.

Journey with Sarah

Sarah holds online containers and circles for mothers to continue their integration and healing within motherhood and womanhood.

You can connect with her on Instagram @sarahholroydhill and her website www.sarahholroydhill.com

Aasta Ryan
Connection As Self-Care

'When you are connected to yourself—really connected to yourself, life feels easier. You know what you need and can gift that to yourself, your intuition is strong, and your relationship with yourself and others just flows.' – Aasta Ryan

Have you ever felt a little lost being a mother? A little too consumed in your family and, or life and felt like there wasn't enough room for you?

Feeling like there wasn't enough room for me, has ebbed and flowed over the years. It first occurred in the haze of new motherhood. However, these feelings arose more recently while navigating toddlerhood, relationships, changing lifestyles by moving to a large property, and delving back into my business.

I wasn't working in early motherhood, and as a full-time Mumma, I felt days and nights melted into one. Time had its own meaning measured between feeds and naps, yet somehow, mysteriously, life still happened outside of that bubble.

I was insanely in love and high on finally becoming a mum, but while I relished the constant skin-on-skin breastfeeding and body napping, I sometimes felt lost. The intense and constant demands of a newborn felt like a lot. I wondered where I began and ended and who I was now outside of being his mother. I often felt so disconnected from myself.

I completed my Kundalini Yoga teacher training while pregnant with my son. After years of practicing in classes weekly, I felt the call to become a teacher. Especially as we were consciously planning on becoming parents, I felt that even if I never taught anyone, it would be one of, if not the most valuable tool to me as a mother, and I was right!

I really wanted to savour every moment of being a new mother, the highs and lows, the ups and downs, but I wanted to feel like I could deal with them instead of drowning in them. To do that, I knew I needed to be grounded and connected, no matter what was happening. And although I found it difficult to carve out chunks of time once the little man arrived, I still managed to maintain a daily Kundalini Yoga practice.

I found a way to stay connected to my highest self and the universe amidst the fog of motherhood, which meant that even on my worst day, I surrendered and trusted, knowing it would all be okay. I knew that what I was moving through would pass, and I was equipped to deal with the big emotions. I knew that whenever I needed to, I could sit on my mat and reconnect in the same way again. I didn't realise it then, but this is how my purpose came about.

Every day I rolled out my yoga mat and lay my son next to or on me, and we would meditate together. I practiced the same mantra I chanted every day while pregnant, and it was so incredible to watch him melt and relax into it just as I did. It was our daily time-out, and it meant for the rest of the day, we were so in tune, so connected to each other, and so in flow that everything just seemed easier.

My little man is now two and a half, and we still practice together. Even though he doesn't sit still and likes to run and jump all over me, he now chants with me at times and loves the closing prayer and blessing. When we practice together, we connect with an energy that means words are less necessary. We just flow and connect to each other and our highest expressions of selves. We seem to 'see' each other very differently. However, with my increasingly busy life, there are times when I wonder how to fit me into this full life. What is me time even? So even though my son and I still practice together, it isn't daily as I feel I need and crave my own sacred connection time.

This practice has been so incredibly nourishing for us to do together, but as my demands, wants, and needs expand again in this new stage of motherhood, I need to be at my best. I need to nourish myself deeply to maintain, healthily, the lifestyle we have created. Connection to myself, the highest version of myself and to the universe means my day flows. I'm not immune to the challenges or emotions that come with life, but it means I am less attached to them. I'm more comfortable letting emotions come and go and releasing them instead of bottling them up. I can see the situation for what it really is instead of the surface-level scenario. Emotions don't cloud me mentally. My body is physically well and able, and my heart and soul feel free to express themselves.

Connection as self-care is everything to me. When I feel connected, I make healthy decisions for myself. I honour my needs instead of ignoring them. I self-regulate big emotions and hold myself, and I hold space for my son and my loved ones. I think more clearly, and I act instead of reacting. I am creative and surrender and trust that everything is working out just as it needs to.

I can't tell you how much more peaceful life is when you feel connected, and connection starts with you. How you feel in yourself flows into every other relationship in your life. The more you develop that connection and relationship with yourself, the more you can see that transformation in all the other relationships in your life, especially with your children!

So, what I would like to share with you, Mumma, is how to implement a daily Kundalini meditation in your own life. You needn't feel daunted that this is a time costly exercise and that it needs a lot from you because it really doesn't, and I hope that this Kundalini Yoga meditation practice will serve you so much that you will want to keep doing it! We all know habits can be tricky to start and maintain, but I promise you this one is worth it!

How Kundalini Yoga can benefit you

Kundalini Yoga is often referred to as the yoga of awareness. It is made up of many different elements, making it unique from other types of yoga. These elements help block out the mental chatter and train your brain to focus. The idea is to shift stagnating energy and balance your energetic and physiological aspects for health, vitality and wellbeing. It is an adjustment for your whole being.

In Kundalini Yoga classes, we first undertake the opening chants, then the Kriya (a set of exercises), Shavasana (relaxation) and then meditation, followed by the closing chants and prayer. In this daily practice setting, we focus on the meditation aspect of Kundalini Yoga, which often includes breathwork, a chant or mantra, specific hand (mudras), and eye (drustis) positions. The idea is to focus the mind on these elements gracefully, without strain or tension and just surrender. At the beginning of each Kundalini Yoga class or practice, it is important to invite in the right energy. This is all part of the connection process. The opening chants connect you to the universe, the highest version of yourself, and all of the great spiritual teachers before you. The chants protect and project your aura and magnetic field from your heart space.

I feel the greatest sense of peace, connection to my heart space, and clarity just from tuning in with these chants. Knowing the vibration the sound of the chant makes is shifting my energy, and the meaning behind each one helps me deeply connect before I have even begun the rest of the practice.

The meditation I am sharing with you uses the mantra 'I AM, I AM'. The first 'I AM' represents your relationship to yourself, the finite expression of who you are. The second 'I AM' represents your relationship to the infinite. Basically, it is a dance that your energy, mind, and being does while posing the question, 'I AM'? and responding with, 'I AM'! Using this chant leaves nothing outside yourself and your truth and your expanding awareness.

Following this meditation is the closing prayer and chant. The Long Time Sun prayer is sung or spoken. It is a beautiful blessing to yourself, followed by the closing chant Sat Nam, which is chanted three times at the end of every Kundalini practice. Sat means truth, and Nam means identity.

The first time it is chanted, it is to bless yourself with the truth of who you are, the second time is to bless everyone you love with their truth, and the third is for everyone in the world. It is such a beautiful extension of energy from you outwards.

Hopefully, you feel that after each part of this practice, knowing the meaning and intention and using the positions and words. What a gift to yourself and, by extension, everyone around you!

This meditation can be practiced any time of the day in any place you feel comfortable but for the best results, do it in the same area between 4am-7am or 4pm-7pm. I am not consistent with the time I do my practice because, well, Mum life! But I do have a little ritual of lighting a candle and rolling out my mat before I do each time.

Start small! In the early newborn days, I sometimes only did a three-minute meditation with the opening and closing chants for about ten minutes. There are still days that is all I get done. Other times, I can do a full Kriya, Shavasana and Meditation.

If you start small, you are less likely to feel overwhelmed with fitting something else in. You can see how such a small commitment can make you feel better, and you will be more inclined to commit more time to it moving forward.

Enjoy!

Aasta Ryan

Part one: The opening chants

ONG NAMO GURU DEV NAMO x 3

Translation:
'I bow to the subtle divine wisdom, the divine teacher within.'

AAD GURAY NAMEH
JUGAAD GURAY NAMEH
SAT GURAY NAMEH
SIREE GUROO DAYVAY NAMEH x 3

Translation:
'I bow to the primal wisdom
I bow to the wisdom true through the ages
I bow to the true wisdom,
I bow to the great unseen wisdom.'

Part two: The meditation

- Sit on the ground with a straight spine and neck extended comfortably. Legs crossed one in front of the other (Easy pose). Alternatively, sit on a straight-back chair.
- The right hand has the thumb and index finger touching at the tip with all the other fingers extended (Gyan Mudra) and the arm straight, resting on the right knee. The left hand is in front of the heart space with the palm facing flat towards the chest and fingers pointing to the right.
- Your eyes are mostly closed and need to be one-tenth open, with your eyes looking straight ahead through your eyelids.
- The left hand starts fifteen centimetres, or six inches, away from

the chest. As you chant aloud, 'I AM', the hand comes closer to the chest, ten centimetres, or four inches.
- While chanting, 'I AM' again, the hand moves out to thirty centimetres, or twelve inches.
- Then take a short breath and bring the hand back to the starting position.
- Create a steady rhythm with the mantra and the breath and continue for three, six, eleven, or thirty-one minutes.

Part three: The prayer and closing chant

You can speak or sing this prayer

May the Long Time Sun Shine Upon You
All love surrounds you
and the pure light within you
guide your way on

SAT NAM x 3

Translation:
'Truth, Truth, I am.'

Come and connect with other mums in our Meditating Mamas Facebook Group, and for pregnant mums, we have a beautiful community in the Becoming Mama Facebook Group.

Aasta Ryan

Aasta is passionate about supporting mothers and mothers to be with the teachings of Kundalini Yoga, Remedial Massage, Baby Massage, Mother Blessingways and more. Aasta believes all mothers should feel supported and held throughout pregnancy, birth and beyond, with the most important being the nourishment of self. Aasta believes that becoming a mother is sacred, and every part of the journey needs to be honoured. Connection and self-care make up a big part of Aasta's teachings, which she believes are essential to not just surviving motherhood but thriving.

Aasta has been a remedial massage therapist for over twenty years. She practised and studied Kundalini Yoga for thirteen years, becoming a teacher three years ago while pregnant with her son. She has spent most of her adulthood utilising natural and alternative therapies and practising Kundalini Yoga, healing her own generational and ancestral trauma, anxiety, stress and PTSD.

Aasta is passionate about sustainable living, lives on a bush block in the Perth Hills, and is a full-time mum to her two and half-year-old son.

Her work and offerings are always evolving, so please see the links below to connect and find out more.

Facebook: https://www.facebook.com/aastaryanlove
Instagram: https://www.instagram.com/aasta_ryan/
Email: love@aastaryan.com

Shani-Faye Chambers
Co-Parenting With Grace

'We pick our parents before we are born to learn the specific lessons our Soul needs for this lifetime. Sometimes we choose supportive parents and lessons, sometimes we choose challenging ones. Our children chose us. Just like we chose our parents.' - Shani Chambers

Would anyone ever really set out to be a single parent? Well, I did it unintentionally. I casually saw a guy I met on Tinder for a couple of months before concluding he wasn't for me. There was no alignment, no future. Our values, morals, and lifestyles were nowhere near on the same page. So, determined to find the love I desperately wanted, I ended it.

A week later, I found out I was pregnant.

I've always firmly believed in old traditions, like marriage before kids, and that starting a family should be a conscious choice made by a committed couple. Preferably when they are at a stage where they are financially prepared.

So naturally, the news I was pregnant hit me like a ton of bricks, and my immediate response was, 'NO WAY! I can't have this child. He's not someone I'd choose for myself, let alone father my children! I need to book an abortion ASAP.'

This response was followed by the loudest and strongest instruction from *Spirit* and intuition I've ever received. 'You need to tell him you are pregnant, and if he wants it, you have this child.'

Ummmmm, What the fuck? Surely this wasn't happening? Surely this isn't what I'd chosen for myself? And as I came up against every piece of resistance, Spirit corrected me each time.

'But I'm not financially secure!'

'Yes, you are, and now you'll make more money than ever before, and you'll be smarter with it.'

'But this is not how I wanted it to happen!'

'This will be beyond perfect. It will be the best thing that ever happens to you.'

'But I don't want to be a single mother. I don't want to be alone in this.'

'You will never feel alone again, and you won't be single forever.'

'But he is not who I'd choose to father my children!'

He will be the perfect father for what this child needs.'

'But I don't want to get faaaaatttttt!' Yes, this one was very emotionally charged.

'You won't. You'll be inspired to take better care of yourself and will even lose weight.'

Ok, so I didn't fully believe most of what came through because I was overcome with fear and doubt, but I knew I couldn't completely ignore what Spirit said, so I told him. Sure enough, he was happy. He had always wanted another child. So it looked like I was having this baby.

Although saying yes to the baby, he immediately became very cold toward me. I was scared. I needed emotional support and to be held. I didn't want to go through this alone. Who would? This is not how I wanted to start a family. I wanted love and someone to nurture me in my vulnerable state. So I started having massive doubts. I didn't want to go through with it. I wanted to wait for what I knew I deserved—a loving man by my side, caring for me through this process.

I reached out to one of my most trusted healers, a great friend and extraordinary intuitive, Devahnah Ellandria. She is gifted in helping new Souls transition onto the Earth, communicating with them quite effectively. I asked her to ask the baby if they'd chosen me and the father. Can I abort and find a new father? Or is this the one they chose?

Sure enough, my baby had chosen this father. She had Karmic Connections and Soul Lessons to complete with him. But, Devahnah assured me it was still my choice. Baby just loves me so much and understands whichever way I choose but assures me if I chose this path, it would be perfect.

So I chose to honour that and bring through this baby.

What was crucial for me in that decision was I had to choose this purely for myself and make sure I could do this entirely on my own. The father hadn't even bothered to ask how I was or if I needed anything. I had to ensure I was one hundred per cent ready to do this without his support, financial, emotional or any other kind. Knowing very little about him, I couldn't go into this if I were relying on him in any way or for anything.

I'm blessed to have so much community support, a great career, close family, and so many beautiful friends. I'm also very resourceful. I realised I didn't need him. As much as I wanted emotional support, I knew I'd never get that from him. So I relied on my tribe for anything and everything I needed. I learned to reach out, and I learned to ask for help. That in itself was such an overdue and powerful lesson.

My amazing business partner, Emma Romano, was a crucial rock of support for me. She said she would move heaven and earth so I could bring this baby through. Emma had my back. She had our business, and thanks to her, I knew I could financially have this baby.

When I told my mother and stepfather, they were so excited. Mum even offered to move in and help me. She assured me they'd be there for me for whatever I needed, and they've never let me down. Mum has always been such an incredible rock of support, so loving, caring, generous and resourceful. My sister really stepped up for me and took quite the delight in throwing the baby shower and even spending the first night with bub and me.

I had my village. I was very blessed. So I knew I could do this without him.

A few weeks later, I started getting the father's messages saying he'd changed his mind. He'd been so cold the whole time, but then he started messing me around. He said he wanted to talk, didn't want to do this, and left me hanging without communication. He even started getting abusive and blaming me. Saying I did it on purpose and that I lied and manipulated him and other nasty things. The old me would have tried to fix things and play the rescuer, which I was so used to doing in relationships.

But becoming a mother changed me. I was learning to honour my needs and my boundaries. So I allowed him to step up and be kind or walk away with no hard feelings. He chose to walk away but missed the no hard feelings part. A few more abusive messages later, I blocked him.

Around twenty-eight weeks, he found a way to contact me. He said he wanted to be a part of his daughter's life and the pregnancy. Despite my feelings toward him, I knew I had to honour my baby's choice. Her Soul chose him from the highest perspective of knowledge of who he is and what he would or would not bring to the table. So, I chose to forgive him and gave him another chance.

He was really kind to us for a while, and I so enjoyed the support he offered. Then he flipped out again just a few weeks before I was due to give birth. Despite how he treated me, I was fully invested in making sure he was a part of my baby's life by this stage. I kept the door open and made sure he was at the birth.

The birth was amazing!

The plan was an induction for medical reasons, but I went into spontaneous labour the minute I laid down for my initial exam. Thirteen hours later, she was born, in the water, with my mum and her dad by my side.

I had never seen him so happy. Her birth changed him deeply. He was kind and supportive again. I still didn't want to be with him romantically, but it was crucial to spend time together so they could bond. We did well for another few months before he flipped again, creating unnecessary drama, being horrible to me and refusing to acknowledge his wrongdoings.

I didn't need to accept that anymore. I had done what I needed to and ensured they had their crucial bonding time when she was too little to be without her mum. It was time to parent separately. It was time to co-parent.

I learnt a lot about navigating this process, ensuring I'm not pulled into repetitive drama triangles and ensuring the handovers and communication are as harmonious as possible for our beautiful daughter.

I learnt to let everything go, not to be offended by anything, not to care what he's projecting at me and not to get upset by any of it. I learnt to keep showing up for myself, setting healthy boundaries from a very diplomatic and non-reactive space. I learned to show him grace, acceptance and appreciation, which softened his energy toward me.

It took a few months before we could get along well, but we settled into a beautiful and respectful co-parenting arrangement. I learnt to be truly grateful for our situation, that Zaalia has a Dad who loves her and wants to be with her and that I get time off from mummying to do things for myself. I'm so glad I learned how to stop the fight and stop the drama. I learnt how to co-parent with grace.

Tips for harmonious co-parenting

It wasn't easy, especially while hormonal and emotionally charged, but these are my top tips for moving into a harmonious co-parenting arrangement.

Navigating Motherhood

Acceptance

One thing you can't change is half your child's DNA. Accepting that if the other parent wants to be in their life, so long as they are not putting the child in danger, we must honour our child's journey. We must nurture that bond with as much love as possible. For our child's sake, at least.

Healing

Crucial to Co-parenting with grace is your ability to remain responsive and non-reactive. Years of healing meant my triggers were very minimal. I didn't take anything personally. However, anytime I was emotionally charged, I could process and move through it rapidly.

Resist the urge to fight

You really do need to pick your battles. Unfortunately, we get anchored into fighting, and if you choose to fight often, the other person will expect a fight and be constantly ready for one, creating more fights. No one wins when we fight. It's important to let the little things go without the need to correct, reprimand or nit-pick.

Gratitude

The best way to get the other parent back onside is to show appreciation. Thank them for their help, even though it should be a given. It's a well-known fact that the more we feel appreciated, the more we give. Hopefully, the more you show appreciation, the more the other parent will show up and eventually reciprocate that appreciation.

Kindness

It's a tough gig, being a parent, even tougher single. The more compassion we show, the more we soften the energies in that relationship. Sending photos of the kids, offering help or support, any opportunity to choose kindness, take it.

Remind the other parent they are doing a great job. It's a wonderful thing to hear.

Drama Triangles

I can't recommend learning this concept highly enough. It's a model that explains all dysfunctional relationships, what's happening within them, how they happen, and how to stop.

Every drama triangle has a Victim, an Aggressor and a Rescuer. As soon as we take on one of those roles, we enter the *Drama Triangle* trap. Once in that triangle, it becomes a merry-go-round.

We constantly swap roles from rescuer to victim to aggressor and around again. No change and no growth happen in this dynamic.

- Refuse to be a victim by having healthy boundaries and self-responsibility.
- Refuse to be the aggressor by healing the reactivity and learning to let things go.
- Refuse to play the rescuer by not jumping in to fix things. It never works.
- Honour yourself first and let others find professional help if they truly want to change.

I might have it easy now, but decades of personal and professional development are what have given me the tools to navigate this tricky path so eloquently. I've walked many difficult paths and turned them all around to be inspirational.

If you feel called to work with me, either privately or in any of my courses, feel free to reach out! I'd love to help you along your journey.

Also, be sure to check out my free training on the Drama Triangle - www.thewellnesschambers.org

Shani-Faye Chambers

- Kinesiologist
- Master Hypnotherapist
- Pranic Psychotherapist
- Multidimensional Energy Healer
- International Spiritual Teacher and Trainer
- Founder of Sacred Ancestral Clearing and DNA Healing
- Co-Founder of The Temple of Divine Intelligence
- Founder of the Wellness Chambers

Shani's journey into the world of healing started at a young age. She was introduced to Reiki and completed her Reiki 1 training when she was ten, which set her up for a life of understanding and working with Energy. A gifted child, Shani struggled a lot emotionally, mentally and spiritually. Spending most of her childhood quite suicidal, she was introduced to Kinesiology when she was fourteen. After two sessions, her entire life changed. No longer struggling, no longer suicidal, Shani realised just how easy healing was when you have the right tools.

Shani-Faye Chambers

A very intuitive Soul, Shani always knew her life path and that she was here for big things. She has been heavily immersed in spiritual training and healing since her late teens. After over a decade of training and overcoming many personal issues, addictions, traumas, sexual abuse, toxic relationships, and body dysmorphia, among other things, she finally opened her doors to see clients professionally in January 2014.

Word spread quickly of the effectiveness and wisdom of Shani's sessions. As a highly sought-after and booked Therapist, Shani rapidly realised she needed to level up again to reach more people. She overcame her fear of public speaking so that her gifts, talents, and healing could spread further.

In 2018, Shani took the stage and shared her story after much healing and preparation. Shani channelled through the Sacred Ancestral Clearing and DNA Healing that put her on the map as an international spiritual teacher. Since then, Shani has channelled through and birthed many New Earth and Ancient Healing Processes and trained over 200 practitioners worldwide both on her own and in her joint venture, The Temple of Divine Intelligence she founded with Emma Romano in 2019.

She is available for private consultations in person and online, as well as short and long workshops, online programs, retreats, practitioner training and mentoring.

She currently lives in Port Kennedy, Western Australia, with her beautiful baby girl and can be reached via her website, www.thewellnesschambers.org

Maryanne Sayers
SLEEP – THE ULTIMATE INGREDIENT

'Sleep is the best meditation.' – Dalai Lam

Big love to you all. I have such an important self-care topic to open up in this chapter, a topic that I love to discuss and that I discuss with mums every day. That topic is sleep.

Self-check on sleep quality

I have a few questions I want you to ponder and ask yourself.

- On a scale of one to ten, one being the worst and ten the best, how rested are you feeling today?
- Are you feeling energised? Are your senses alive, and are you feeling alert?
- Are you feeling sluggish or tired? Do you feel like you are going through your day under a cloud of fog?
- Think about how rested you feel overall, not just today but every day. What would that number be on a scale of one to ten? Some further questions will provide you with a top-line insight into

the quality of your sleep patterns. What time do you go to bed at night?
- Are you able to go to sleep quickly, or do you lie awake for hours?
- Do you frequently wake through the night?
- Do you toss and turn and generally have a very interrupted sleep? Are you sleeping solidly and deeply and not waking up until morning ready to start your day?

These are important self-care reflections, and if you take a few minutes to think about these questions properly, you will know deep down within yourself if your sleep is in good shape or not.

Video games to baby sleep

As a baby sleep consultant and educator, it's fair to say that sleep is my jam. However, I haven't always been a baby sleep specialist. In fact, if someone told me twenty years ago this is what I would be doing, it would have made no sense to me that a career path in baby sleep was in my future.

Let me share my back story, which led me here. I was in corporate land in the 1990s and early 2000s, working in a senior management role in the video games industry…Nintendo, anyone? My first child, Bethany, was born in 2004. Like many first-time parents, I struggled with her sleep.

I couldn't get her to sleep easily. She woke frequently, and she was very unsettled. I was exhausted and completely at the end of my tether. I had never experienced sleep deprivation like it. It was bloody awful, if I'm honest, and it impacted my experience of motherhood. I had no idea what to do or how to get her to sleep well. Everyone I asked and everything I read told me something different.

To cut a long story short, I sought help and intervention with her sleep. I was fortunate to be given the correct education on baby sleep at the time, which completely changed my life. Finally, I had the right understanding and realised that nearly everything I had thought about baby sleep was just not right.

Everything I tried to put into practice with her was working against her natural sleep cycles and body clock. I was unwittingly caught up in complete information overload from various resources, books, well-meaning family and friends and even my GP, but all of it conflicted, and none of it was consistent.

Suddenly, once I properly understood, everything made sense, and I saw that sleep was one of the most natural things in the world for my baby. The simplicity of it all was a revelation. When you have the correct understanding of something, life becomes infinitely easier!

As a result of my personal experience, I wanted to share my new knowledge. I knew helping mums and families was my calling, and I wanted to help as many as possible. I wanted to simplify sleep for babies and children.

Simplifying sleep

Sleep is a fundamental human function. It's nature. It's biology. We are all designed to sleep and sleep well. It all comes back to the foundations, which apply to all of us, babies, toddlers, children, teenagers and adults. All of us!

Alongside nutrition and exercise, sleep is one of the three pillars for optimum health and wellness. I help mums achieve great, natural, consistent sleep patterns with their baby or toddler every day, equating to great sleep for the mums.

We have this amazing nature clock, known as our body clock, which is driven by our circadian rhythm. Circadian rhythm recurs, regulating our sleep, feed and wake cycles in a natural and beautifully consistent pattern that moves between sleeping and being awake. I definitely agree with this next quote.

'A good laugh and a long sleep are the two best cures for anything.' - Old Irish proverb

Your baby's sleep

If you are a mother of a baby or young child, I know that for many of you, you aren't getting anywhere near the amount of sleep that you should be getting.

With newborns and young babies, of course, our nighttime sleep is interrupted because newborns and young babies require feeding overnight. However, the lack of sleep I'm talking about here, which I know affects thousands of families everywhere, far exceeds just getting up a couple of times each night to feed your baby.

I'm talking about sustained, chronic sleep deprivation, where your baby wakes multiple times each night, leading to broken sleep and frequent wakings for you and your baby. Both of you are caught in the same overtired cycle every day. It's not natural for the human body to be overtired and exhausted. Sustained sleep deprivation is not a normal state to be in, not for babies and not for adults.

'There is no baby on this earth who hates sleep.' – Maryanne Sayers

The foundations of sleep

Sleep truly is an essential fuel for our health and well-being. It plays a critical role in immune function, metabolism, memory, learning, and other vital functions. We will survive with poor, fractured sleep patterns, but we will thrive with great, consistent sleep patterns the way nature intended.

I would like to share some essential sleep foundations that we all need to know. And here's the thing, the same foundational elements that apply to us as adults also apply to our babies and children's sleep. The foundations of sleep are the same for everyone!

Positive mindset on sleep

Having a positive mindset about sleep is the first foundation I discuss with families. It's important to shift your thinking from sleep as being 'hard work' and telling yourself, 'My baby hates sleep' or that 'My sleep will always be bad' to a healthier mindset.

Instead, tell yourself, 'Sleep is a fundamental need for all of us, and I need to reset the current processes, rituals and cycles I'm caught in and focus on the big-picture foundations.'

Understand that fundamentally, babies, children, and adults want to sleep easily and well. Like eating and breathing, sleep is an incredibly natural biological function and process of our amazing bodies.

> 'Sleep is like the golden chain that binds our health and body together.' – Thomas Dekker

Responding to tired signs

In a nutshell, the really straightforward understanding around this is that when humans are tired, they will always feel tired and display signs of tiredness. When we are overtired, our body's natural response to that tiredness is to want to go to sleep.

When we are too overtired, we are over-stimulated, making it challenging to relax down into sleep and drift off easily. This is a particular issue for babies and young children who fall into cycles of being overtired, leading to escalated crying and unsettled behaviour.

Key points for tired signs

If you are feeling tired and lethargic during the day or simply feeling irritable from tiredness, take a nap or a rest if there is an opportunity.

With babies and toddlers, tired signs are easily identified once you know what to look for.

Signs of being tired include yawning, rubbing eyes, irritability, clinginess, and a sense that you always need to pick them up and hold them to avoid crying and whingeing.

For daytime naps, be guided by your baby's cues rather than following awake times pre-determined by the clock. This leads to being overtired very quickly because often, children are tired well before a predetermined awake time has lapsed. Again, be guided by your baby, not the clock.

If you are feeling tired, then you are tired. If your baby looks and sounds tired, then your baby is tired. The tired signs never lie!

Sleep environment

For any of us to sleep well, we must have the right sleep environment. If we are too warm or cold, if the room has too much light, or if it's too noisy, if the bed isn't comfortable, it will negatively impact our sleep.

Tips on sleep environments

- Avoid artificial lights or noise in the sleep environment, like white noise and night lights.
- Ensure a dark room for night-time.
- A firm, comfortable mattress for your bed and the mattress in your baby's cot or bassinet.
- Ensuring babies and toddlers have a safe sleeping space is important. Don't have any bedding or loose items in their cot or bassinet. Just a mattress with a fitted sheet is enough.
- Adequate warmth is essential for cooler nights. Frequent wakings will occur if our babies are not warm enough for the night.

The best kind of sleep environment for our babies and for us is a simple one.

It really is!

Appropriate bedtime

As adults, we all choose our own bedtime. It's a personal choice, a lifestyle choice. Many adults declare that they don't need a lot of sleep. However, if our adult body clocks could talk, every single one of those body clocks would say, 'We need eight to nine hours of sleep every night.' What we think we need versus what we actually need are often two very different things.

In the same way, if you were to speak to the body clocks of our babies and toddlers, their body clocks would say, 'We need twelve to thirteen hours of sleep at night.'

Having the right bedtime is important for adults, babies and children to align with their naturally occurring sleep, feed and wake cycles. Essentially, it's about lining up the daytime and nighttime with the natural circadian rhythm and the bedtimes that our body clocks are trying to tap into. For many, we underestimate the amount of sleep that babies, children and adults actually need every twenty-four hours.

Bedtimes for body clocks

- For adults, a bedtime around 9.30pm to 10.30pm is ideal to start the day between 6am, and 7am.
- Older toddlers and preschool children need bedtime around 6.30 pm to start the day between 6am, and 7am.
- Babies and younger toddlers need a bedtime of 6pm Anything later than 6pm is an enormously long day for a baby—too long. And they go into the overtired zone very quickly.

Getting enough sleep is so important for you and your baby. Fundamentally, this begins with having an appropriate bedtime.

Your baby's sleep begins here

I hope my insights into sleep have been helpful. Remember that the foundations of good, healthy sleep habits are the same for all of us, whether babies, children or adults. Prioritising sleep is one of the most important self-care practices we can do for our mind, body and soul.

Focusing on your own sleep is the first step to resolving your baby or toddler's sleep issues, which is one hundred per cent where I can help you. Please reach out, and set up a consultation with me. You can find my contact details in my bio below.

'A happy, engaged and well-rested baby equals a happy, engaged and well-rested mother.' - Maryanne Sayers

Maryanne Sayers

Maryanne Sayers is one of Australia's leading baby and toddler sleep experts. She's helped thousands of families by providing parents with the right education, knowledge and understanding of baby sleep. Maryanne bases her education on getting back to basics and teaches people to have a big-picture understanding surrounding the foundations of infant sleep.

Maryanne is a certified Maternity and Child Sleep Consultant, completing her diploma-level studies with the IHPI (International Health and Parenting Institute). She is also a member of the APSC (Association of Professional Sleep Consultants). She was recently appointed as Australia's official Baby Sleep Expert for Kidspot.

Maryanne has been featured in various national Australian media and is also a frequent guest speaker and contributor on many community parenting forums and at parenting seminars. In 2019, Maryanne was invited as a Keynote International Speaker to attend the 2019 Starfish Lane Nursery Toddler Health and Wellness Conference in Doha, Qatar, in the Middle East.

Maryanne Sayers

Maryanne provides one-on-one consultations to families via phone or video call and has recently released an online baby sleep program.

Contact details:

Maryanne Sayers

Baby Sleep Educator

Ph: (61) 2 417 068 545

Website: https://maryannesayers.com.au

Facebook: https://www.facebook.com/MaryanneSayersBabySleepConsultant

Instagram @maryannesayers1

Kara Williams
Cultivating Healthy Habits

'Healthy habits are the small things we repeat daily that lead us to our ideal life, to satisfaction, to true joy.' - Kara Grace

I wanted to be a mother for as long as I can remember. In high school, my nickname was 'Mum', not only because my friends knew how desperately being a mother was my life goal but also because of the way I nurtured those around me.

My dreams became a reality, and I sat cradling my bump and fantasising about what life would be like. Along with dealing with swollen ankles, nausea and terrible back pain, let's be honest, we don't all get the pregnancy glow and glide through like Miss Mumma Universe.

Carrying around that bump, I was full of pride, joy and gratitude. It was such a blessing because I was unsure if I could carry my own child and through the whole process, the good and the bad, gratitude and the care people offered sustained me.

But then things changed.

I left the hospital, which is terrifying for any new parent, but I quickly realised I needed help. *Actual* help. This was more than new mumma nerves.

My dreams and fantasies were a whole lot different to the reality I was now living. I didn't have family and friends close by that could just 'drop in', and as I turned to the professional world, I felt lonelier than ever, misunderstood, frustrated and helpless.

With a history of serious mental illness, I finally mustered up the courage to talk to my new doctor because I realised that not only had I relapsed, but it had intensified. This is where I truly felt the gap in our system. The disregard for mothers. The realisation that all care was baby centred. The societal expectations are that we sacrifice *everything* for our children, no matter what, and that is what makes us good mothers.

I left that appointment with no support but a script for antibiotics 'in case I was sick'. I left broken and defeated. Everything I ever wanted was falling to pieces. My screams for help filled nothing but an empty void.

In hindsight, I now realise this was complete medical negligence. Thankfully, my husband never left my side. He pulled me through and helped me fight when I felt like I couldn't until I received the help I needed. The help I deserved. The help that we, as mothers, shouldn't have to fight for.

I was more determined than ever to give our girl and future family the best life possible. This is where I passionately began obsessively reading about holistic health and wellness. I focused all my energy and attention on natural, holistic, preventative approaches in an attempt to avoid the traditional approach to only treating symptoms.

And I did it!

Each week there were one-to-two small changes. Each week there was something we did differently. Each month there was a noticeable change, and each year, a complete overhaul. We took it step-by-step. We made it realistic and achievable. We focused on healthy habits. We did small things repeated daily that led us to our ideal life—to health, wellness, joy and utter contentment.

Eventually, my own research was not enough to satisfy the inner learner in me. I also grew more and more passionate about being a voice for other mummas. After being let down by so many professionals, I knew I couldn't be the only one. But I also knew I could help be the change—I needed to be the change. I knew it was actually possible to cultivate healthy habits in motherhood and not sacrifice our own well-being for the sake of our families. But I also knew that I needed a legitimate certification behind me. So, I enrolled to study at the Institute of Integrative Nutrition.

A few years later, armed with my new qualifications, determination and passion, Kara Grace Collective was birthed. A whole new baby—my Holistic Women's Health Coaching Business.

I now work with busy mums with young children to fill the gap. I help them prioritise their time, know their worth and value, and get organised, so they have time and space for what is important. Time and space to look after themselves. Time and space, so they don't burn out. Time and space to *enjoy* their life, not *endure* it. Time and space to be proactive and not reactive about their families health and wellbeing.

So the question is, Mumma, do you want this kind of life?

If you are ready for change, ready to look after yourself and not just your family, the best place to start is by cultivating healthy habits—repeated small changes that add up to a whole new way of life.

Guide to cultivating healthy habits

One: Reflect

But wait, why do I need to think about the past? Isn't this all about future thinking?

Well, here is the thing, we need to look back, reflect, process and hold space before we can truly move forward in an authentic and healthy way that will have longevity in our life.

When we reflect, we want to make sure we consider the negatives *and* the positives. We have a safe, quiet, comfortable space. We get ready to be open and vulnerable with ourselves. We have a way to process—write, journal, sing, create art. Whatever it may be, you need a way to process. If you are new to this, I highly recommend starting with journaling.

Ask yourself these questions when journalling

- What has been going really well?
- Why has it been going so well?
- What can I do to ensure this area of my life keeps going well?
- What has not been going well?
- Why has it not been going well?
- When did it start? Was there a single event, or was it building up?
- What do I want this to look like?
- Who can help me?
- What support do I need?
- What will it look like and feel like when this area of my life starts to go well?
- What does my ideal life look like? What does it feel like? Who is in it, and who is removed from it?
- If all limitations were removed, I would …

So grab a pen and a journal and spend some time in this space. You might spend a few hours and wrestle with it or spend short periods over several days or weeks on it. Just don't take longer than four weeks. There is no right or wrong way to do this. The only rule is to be vulnerable and honest with yourself.

Two: Plan

Okay, now you know what is important to you, what is going well and what needs improving, you are ready to plan.

The planning stage is about mapping out how you can practically integrate healthy habits and rhythms into your life. For example, if you want to eat more nutritious home-cooked meals, you need to create space in your week to do meal planning and meal prep.

Do you want to exercise even though you have the kids around? Change your daily routine so you can do it together in the morning when they are refreshed from sleep and happily fed after breakfast.

Do you want more time to allocate to meditation and journaling? If you are a morning person, set your alarm half an hour earlier and do it before the rest of the household wakes up. Or, if you are an evening person, instead of turning on the television as soon as the kiddos are in bed, have your quiet time.

For your planning stage, you must map out how you will practically achieve your goals for your planning stage.

Follow these simple steps

- Have a weekly template. I call this your *Ideal Week*.
- First, write out everything you have to do and cannot change. Think about things like school drop-off, work, swimming lessons.
- Now go back to your list of what you want to start prioritising. Was it meditation, nutritious cooking, or more exercise? Whatever it was, it is time to prioritise the important thing in your week. Find a space where it will fit, write it in and make it a habit. Make it part of your weekly rhythms.

Lastly, and possibly the most important and hardest, get up every day, look at your plan and commit to doing it. Mumma, you've got this!

Three: Start small

It is completely unrealistic to start doing everything at once. As a busy mumma juggling everything life throws us, we set ourselves up for failure if we think we can become a meditating, journaling, meal-prepping mumma in five days.

Have a look at the plan you just created. What is most important to you? Start with that. Remember, healthy habits are the small things we repeat daily. So if you want to start eating less take-out and eating more nutritious home-cooked food, focus on meal planning. Do this consistently for four weeks, and find your rhythm. Initially, you might have thought meal planning on a Monday night was best for you, but then you may find that doesn't work. You trial a few other nights and realise that meal planning on a Friday morning works best for you. Once you find your flow with this, focus on your next priority.

Four: Regularly check in with yourself

We could have the best-written plan, but if it doesn't practically work for you and your life, it is a complete waste. There is a difference between intentions and reality. You don't have to change your goals, but you might have to change how you achieve them. That is why it is so important to check in regularly with yourself.

Keep up your habit of journaling. Each week write down what went well and why it went well. Consider what didn't go well and why. Allow yourself time to think about how you can make small adjustments to your habits and rhythms to make it work.

The key to success

Cultivating healthy habits is possible for all of us, regardless of our history or our current position. But making the change is hard. It is not one size fits everyone. There is no magic formula we can all do and suddenly become these amazing mamas who have it all together, forget nothing and live in constantly organised bliss.

Ralph Waldo Emmerson once said, 'It's not the destination, it's the journey.' Along the way, we refine and adjust according to the season of life we are in.

It can feel overwhelming to do this alone. I know this all too well. It is overwhelming to know which is the right approach for us, having the grit to stick with it in the tough times and feeling supported, uplifted and encouraged. It was from this place that I birthed The Organised Family—a six-session program for busy mums.

The Organised Family has the flexibility, and affordability mummas need to fit in with their life situations. Pay upfront or pay in instalments. Do your six sessions weekly, fortnightly or monthly and do your six sessions online, according to your time zone.

The Organised Family gives you all the expert information, tools and personalised support to help you cultivate healthy habits and a life you enjoy, not just endure! In the six sessions, we deep dive into my Four-Step Guide to Cultivating Healthy Habits, plus more.

As a mama, our time and money are so precious. Before jumping in to work with you, I always do a free initial call. This allows us both to make an informed choice. We can decide if I am the right person to help you on your journey. Make sure you book your free call with me on my website.

Kara Williams

Kara Williams is the founder of the Kara Grace Collective: The Organised Family. She is a Holistic Health Coach and works with busy and overwhelmed mums with young kids to help them prioritise their time, get organised, achieve their goals and be confident in who they are and their purpose.

Kara specialises in helping mothers

- Create routines
- Meal plans and meal prep
- Get their budget under control
- Transition to a low toxic lifestyle
- To help women know and understand their strengths and purpose in motherhood and beyond.

Kara believes motherhood should be enjoyed, not endured. She understands each person and life situation is different and unique. Therefore, she does not have a *one size fits all* approach. All consults and resources are personalised and individualised. She understands mums need simple strategies that are family-friendly and won't break the budget.

Kara holds a Bachelor of Education and a Health Coach Certification through the Institute of Integrative Nutrition and has developed her specialised, signature six-session program, The Organised Family, which is now available a limited of times per year in an online format or for one-on-one sessions. Sessions are completed online, and she accommodates your time zone. Find out more on her website www.karagracecollective.com.

Connect with Kara
Email: hello@karagracecollective
Website: www.karagracecollective.com
Instagram: @karagrace_co - www.instagram.com/karagrace_co
Facebook: Kara Grace Collective - www.facebook.com/karagraceco
YouTube: The Organised Family - https://www.youtube.com/channel/UCGilQe-rwZMRopDTAsPuG1A

Kelly Lam
Align Your Life

'When you allow yourself to be who you are, not who the world wants you to be, then you have more of yourself to share with your children and others.'
- Kelly Lam

I tried to be who the world wanted me to be my whole life. I was an obedient girl growing up. I listened to my parents and did what they asked. They had a vision for me to do well in school and get into university so I could get a good job in an office and have a good life. Their vision is what I worked toward as a little girl. I wanted to make them proud.

I achieved all that. I received first-class honours at university. I was proud of myself, and my parents were proud of me. I got into a graduate role for a global I.T. company and worked in an office. Life was going according to plan.

Until I fell pregnant in my early twenties with my first boyfriend's baby, and life changed dramatically. I became a wife, moving in with my husband. Soon after, my first child was born. That was when I experienced the real world because my parents no longer looked after me. Instead, I had my own family to look after, including a newborn baby.

Navigating Motherhood

Suddenly, I was thrown into the deep end. Nothing I knew prepared me for motherhood. Being faced with multiple challenges all in one go, I was being stretched to the max, mentally, emotionally and physically.

I tried to figure out how to do motherhood and life, but I was sleep deprived, and no time for myself was now the *norm*. I soon realised that what the world told me about how I should care for and raise my baby did not always work for me. So, I learned to surrender and do what worked for me.

My priorities had changed. I no longer wanted to return to the same I.T. role after a year of maternity leave. Instead, I wanted to give my baby the best gift of health I could. So I decided to breastfeed for as long as I was able. People told me it was silly, I wasn't doing the best for my baby, and my milk wasn't as good after the first year. But I was resolute.

However, I wanted to work but didn't see myself working five days a week in a job I may be on-call on weekends. So I reached out to my manager and expressed my concerns. Luckily, they offered me a part-time admin role.

Life was going well. I believed I had a *perfect* life. I truly loved my husband, I had my little boy, and we were expecting another baby. My husband and I did our best to care for our children together. However, my relationship with my husband wasn't how I expected. The pressure built up, and I was drowning in life's busyness, trying to juggle everything and keep on top of life. I found myself crumbling down and hitting rock bottom multiple times.

'Many of us have learned to be who the world wants us to be. But there comes a time when it is harder to hold onto this façade than it is to embrace who we truly are. To surrender to how we have changed and align life to that way of being.' – Rebecca Campbell

Even if you marry the man you love the most, happily ever after is an illusion. There is no *perfect* life and definitely no *perfect* relationship. Motherhood is *hard*. Relationships are *hard*. Life is *hard*! I learnt that sometimes struggles are needed so we can understand, love and accept ourselves for who we are and allow ourselves to live a life true to us.

One day I had a conflict with my husband. I felt so sad and wanted to run away from my life. However, my two little kids stopped me. So instead of running away from my life, I ran away to the city and attended a free event called The Turning Point Intensive. This event was a pivotal moment in my life.

What I realised was, until that moment, I had never asked my husband to look after the kids on his own for a whole day. I also realised that being a mother was one of my excuses for why I couldn't take time away to do things for myself. I always felt like I had to be there for the kids.

I was trying to live up to the *social norm* of what a good mother should be—the one that always puts her kids first and herself last. So, my struggles and hitting rock bottom multiple times in my relationship became the catalyst for my growth and transformation, leading me on a journey of self-discovery. Now I'm a Certified Results Coach, and I'm well on my way to building my *own* version of success in life, both as a mother and as the woman I want to be.

I discovered more about myself and my values and learned that when I stop trying to live by other people's values or society's expectations, I can choose what I *really* want and consciously create a life that feels good to me.

> *'A lot of conflict you have in your life exists simply because you're not living in alignment; you're not being true to yourself.'* – Steve Maroboli

So, if you want true fulfilment and happiness in your life, you have to live a life according to your *own* highest values. That's when you live a life true to you.

Navigating Motherhood

This doesn't mean life will be smooth sailing when you find fulfilment. It simply means that because you know what is important to you and have identified your priorities, you can make better decisions for yourself according to your values. Creating boundaries to protect your time and energy will become so much easier.

I discovered from my personal journey and experience as a Certified Results Coach that for us mothers to be who we are and not who the world wants us to be, we first need to make ourselves a priority. We must discover our true selves, which have been lying dormant under the needs and wants of everyone else. Then align our life so we can be ourselves and be the mother we want to be.

Self-care is essential

> *'It all begins with you. If you do not take care of yourself, you will not be strong enough to take care of anything in life.'* – Leon Brown

Early in my motherhood journey, I quickly fell into the trap of *no me time* as I devoted most of my days and nights to my family's needs. As a result, self-care wasn't even on my radar. I was busy doing too much, but I felt like I wasn't doing enough because I didn't get to do things that were for me.

I want to tell you that if you are tired, run-down and overwhelmed, you will not be able to take good care of your children or anyone else. Self-care does not have to be complicated and take a lot of time. It can simply be making sure you drink enough water every day and have enough sleep so you can be your best self. Sometimes when you have less time, the little moments you take for yourself make a difference in how you feel.

So remember to create time out of your busy life to focus on yourself. Not only will you be in a better state to take care of others, but you will feel like you again.

What activities can you do for yourself today that will make you feel nourished?

Your own values or someone else's

Whenever you find yourself using the words 'should…I ought to…I have to' it indicates that you are doing it because of someone else's values.

When you are not doing what you should be doing, you end up experiencing what Dr John Demartini said, '…are the *ABCD's* of negativity- anger, blame, criticism, and despair, directed toward yourself.' The pain of the ABCDs of negativity actually reveals to you how out of touch you are with your true self.

Signs you're living by your own highest values are when you hear yourself saying things such as 'I love doing this…I'm inspired by doing that…I dream of doing this… I choose and live to do this.'

So, be conscious of the words you use next time!

Know your values

> *'It's not hard to make decisions once you know what your values are'*
> *– Roy E. Disney*

Values are anything you consider important to you, and they can certainly change throughout your life. For example, when you are aged zero to ten, your values may be playing and fun. But you grow, and now you're aged between ten and twenty, and your values are now social interaction and friendship. However, when you're in your twenties and thirties, it may be establishing a relationship, career or creating financial foundations.

It is important to find out what your highest values are because they're the driving force for living a life that's true to you. For example, my family became my highest value when I had kids, so going back to work full-time no longer felt good to me. Then through motherhood and life,

I experienced financial and relationship struggles that led me to realise freedom, wealth, connection and love are now some of my highest values. Becoming conscious of your values will help you make decisions that lead you to create an inspired and fulfilling life.

You can find a link in my bio for a quiz by Dr John Demartini that can help you discover what some of your core values are.

Eliminate mum guilt

One of my mentors, Benjamin J. Harvey, said, 'Your life demonstrates your value conflicts until the conflicts are removed, and once they are removed then it demonstrates your values.'

This means we often want to do or have something in our life but feel like we can't because of something else that we see is important. Hence, there is an internal conflict between two things of equal importance. As mums, our children and family are one of our highest values, so we often find ourselves in situations where we can't do what we want because we feel bad or guilty for not being there for our children and family. Unless we can remove the conflict by making the connection in our brain of how one thing can help the other, we will always feel frustrated when we can't do what we love the most.

For example, I want to take a two-day holiday with my girlfriends at the weekend but I can't because of my children.

A simple process I go through to resolve this is I ask myself this question multiple times, 'How will going on a holiday for the weekend help me spend more time with my children?'

This question may not make sense because my brain can't see a connection, to begin with. This is normal. This disconnect creates conflict between going on holiday with my girlfriends and spending time with my children. The key is to persist and ask the same question repeatedly, forcing the brain to come up with multiple answers to create a new-neural pathway connecting the two values.

Another simple question to ask ourselves is, 'How will what we want benefit our children and family?' Then let our brains be creative and come up with multiple answers. Again, persist with this process and keep going until you have different possible answers to the question. Don't overthink when going through this process. Trust whatever comes up is the right answer for you. When resolved, you will have no more mum's guilt and no more internal conflict between two opposing values that prevent you from doing what you love the most.

You are a gift

'Values are like fingerprints. Nobody's are the same, but you leave 'em all over everything you do.' – Elvis Presley

We all have our own unique set of values because we are all different. It's important to know that even when you become a mum, you are allowed to be who you want to be. You certainly don't need to try and fit into what you believe is society's norm of *motherhood*.

When you get to know yourself, learn to love yourself. Allow yourself to be who you really are. Do things that bring you joy, and that is when you will show your children the importance of living a life true to themselves.

Surround yourself with support

'Life doesn't make any sense without interdependence. We need each other, and the sooner we learn that, the better for us all.' – Erik H. Erikson

Lastly, you don't need to do motherhood and life alone. It's okay to ask for help and support whenever you need it. It's important to find your tribe and have a community of like-minded women or mums that you connect with and who will support you in your journey.

Navigating Motherhood

If you are looking to create a fulfilling life that aligns with your values so you can be the mother and woman you want to be, then as a Certified Results Coach, I can help guide and support you.

I want to close this chapter by reminding you that you are important too!

Only when you allow yourself to be who you are, not who the world wants you to be, then you will have more of yourself to share with your children and others.

Kelly Lam

Kelly Lam is a Certified Results Coach, a business mentor, a speaker, an author and a mother of four who made it her mission to inspire, guide and support mothers to live in their truth and be their most authentic selves.

Kelly believes true happiness comes from within and can only be achieved when you decide to embrace yourself and take control of your life instead of settling for the norm. Her satisfaction comes from helping women step confidently into their authentic power and levelling up all areas of their lives, so they are fulfilled being the mother and women they want to be.

Currently, she has aligned herself with an online holistic health program with the opportunity to create residual income streams. She sees this as a vehicle to help her clients live their best lives. Because she believes wealth is an important asset. Without it, your health and relationships can be affected.

You can can work with Kelly through her coaching program, Kelly can help you rediscover yourself and start creating a life that feels good to you, where you can do the things you love and be a great mother at the same time.

To claim your free *'Rediscover You'* session, go to https://www.kellylam.com.au/freesession

Kelly is equally as passionate about helping you create your own income from home that fits around your family, as she knows how hard life is when we don't have enough and just get by.

She would love you to connect with her online to see her latest offers.

Website: https://www.kellylam.com.au/
Facebook: https://www.facebook.com/kellylamcoach
Instagram:
https://www.instagram.com/kellylam.coach/
Email: info@kellylam.com.au
Dr John Demartini, Value Determination Process link:
https://drdemartini.com/values/

Nathalie Biviano
Nurturing Your Marriage

Nurturing Your Marriage is Nurturing Yourself – Nathalie Biviano
'The quality of our lives is determined by the quality of our relationships.' – Esther Perel

How did we end up here? You know when you've been at home all day with the crying baby, and you tip a max threshold where you just can't deal with a crying baby anymore? And he just doesn't get it? Hurtful words get thrown like daggers, and you get so emotionally hijacked that you're completely immobilised.

Have you ever been at such a low point? We loved each other, but after the baby, we didn't feel *loved* by each other.

More on this a bit later.

Transitions no baby books talk about

The greatest shock of motherhood? The emotional evaporation between my husband and me. I aim to illustrate how unprepared I was for this grand impact on marriage. Whether single or in a heterosexual or same-sex marriage, this chapter should help you deepen relationships in your life. After all, what is life without quality relationships?

Navigating Motherhood

Nurturing marriage is self-care

Nurturing and protecting marriage is self-care. Like an insurance policy, you need an external buffer to protect you when you rage at each other. Similar to a car, house or health insurance, there's a third party to cushion you if things go south. But you can't *purchase* marriage insurance; you can only build the buffer yourself. Making deposits of *emotional equity* in the *Emotional Bank Account*, a term coined by Dr John Gottman. An *emotional bank account* is strategic emotional self-care; it bubble wraps you when you need it.

Flying high in love: A backstory

Before I circle back to the hurtful daggers story, let me give you some tiny snippets of our love for context. Before kids, my husband put me on a pedestal. We went on long-dreamy motorbike rides around The Rocks in Sydney. He took me on weekend getaways to Callala Bay on the NSW South Coast. For our first Valentine's Day, he booked a helicopter ride. We went to dinner twice a week with his mum. He'd get little surprises when he filled up at the petrol station. He'd charge my phone every night and call me every morning as my alarm like a personal concierge service—total bliss.

We met in Punchbowl, Sydney, in 2005. I worked in marketing, and he was a mechanic. I tapped keyboards, and he turned spanners. While our crafts were worlds apart, our magnetic connection was sparked by humour and aligned, Sicilian and Cambodian family values.

One night I worked late to finish a presentation. He brought dinner and sat with me while I did my *PowerPoint*. As someone who types with one finger, his pupils dilated with marvel seeing me utilise keyboard shortcuts. 'Wow, you really know what you're doing,' he said, not in a pissing-yer-pocket way. It was genuinely sincere. It made me feel capable and adored. It felt gooey and marshmallowy. I felt seen and deeply loved.

A year into our relationship, I scored the *crème de la crème* marketing role based in London, with frequent travel to New York. Carrie vibes! Big apple! A dream come true! I was so proud of myself for achieving this goal and mopped up every piece of congratulatory praise. 'Look at you, ya jet setter!' I loved how accomplished and important it made me feel. Once again, it felt gooey and marshmallowy, and I felt seen and deeply loved.

But the truth was, my passion for my job diminished. And being away from him ached. On my last New York City trip, as I ordered yet another room service for one, my soul's whisper became louder than the adrenalin of Times Square. I am so damn lonely. This job is sucking my soul. I want to go back home to Australia.

I was back in the arms of my lover and back to the drawing board. While I felt lost, I always had his support. For a man of few words, he always knew what to say. Funny how chatterboxes are attracted to the quiet ones. I felt protected. I went back to the corporate world but in a different industry. I learned new skills and made amazing lifelong friends, but ultimately concluded that corporate life suffocated me. Fast forward a few years, and I finally had an *out*. I became pregnant at twenty-nine. New parenting adventures with my beloved!

Didn't know words could be daggers

Okay, I'm circling back to that moment. Allow me to set the scene. Our daughter was six months old, and we'd recently started our business. We bickered a lot. He worked big hours. My thoughts were, *How can I help him?*

I wanted to lessen his burden. I leveraged freelancing with my skills. One day, I was keen to finish a project so I could invoice it. I had an unsettled-crying baby on my shoulder and a laptop balanced on my knee. I was impossibly multitasking, so I popped her down. She continued crying. The husband's truck pulled up. The gate opened. He's close enough to hear her crying. I was desperate for him to see how much I wanted to help financially. He walked in and saw his precious princess unattended, in distress and saw me on my laptop. He exploded! I can't even remember the words. All I remember was it was enough to annihilate my spirit emotionally. He crushed me to the core.

That night, I curled into a foetal position, fractured from the hurt of his words, and just cried. As I sniffed and sucked back the dribbling snot, I closed my eyes and quietly protested, 'This is not how it's supposed to be.'

'There are two types of couples: The Disasters and The Masters of relationship.'
– Dr John Gottman

Rock bottom: The impetus for improvement

I decided to be a master. Mastery is the mindset to be a student every day. Over ten years, I've poured time, energy and money into books, programs, coaching and podcasts on marriage mastery. Now, hand on my heart, I've truly curated my nirvana life—a life that makes my soul sing. I live my *dharma* as I coach other mamas to create love in their marriages and life. It feels exquisite.

Here are some thoughts, ideas and concepts about marriage that have given big emotional yield—small movements, big changes. The embodiment of these ideas is also known as living my *martial code of conduct*.

Decode his expressions of love

His love language is acts of service and gifts. His deepest desire was for me to care for our baby. Seeing me choose the laptop over our precious girl was a dagger piercing his heart.

My love language is words of affirmation. Notice when I was affirmed I felt loved? 'Good job! Wow, look at you.' The night he exploded, I translated his words as 'You're a complete failure', which is why I crumbled.

5 Love Languages, by Gary Chapman, is a game changer, a must-read. Here are some things I've decoded since reading his book.

Instead of:	It becomes:
'He's always at work.'	'Gosh, he loves me'
'This car is a waste of cash.'	'Gosh, he loves me'
'Just pay the lawn guy!'	'Gosh, he loves our home'

It's a balance between 'Oh, that's him showing me love' and asking for what I need by saying, 'Hey babe, here's what would be more meaningful.'

Ask for what I need

He's not a mind reader. Learning to ask for my needs took time and practice. Also, I had to learn to be compassionate with his *bandwidth* to deliver what I needed.

For a long time, I craved *orange juice, orange juice, orange juice*. 'But I'm an apple,' he would whisper.

Honour differences between Mars and Venus

It distils down to men needing respect and women needing to be emotionally understood.

Alison Armstrong, a famous author and relationship expert, theorises that women get it wrong in relationships because they think that men are 'hairy women misbehaving.' I ate lots of humble pie when I examined how much I emasculated him by eye-rolling. Emasculation equals disrespect.

Am I in my feminine?

Marriage needs polarity. When we're both in *masculine mode*, do and produce results, tension rises because we're out of balance. The dynamic collapses until one of us embodies *feminine vibes*, like patience, joy and creativity.

Transitioning to *feminine energy* can take up to twenty minutes. So, from 2.30pm, I switch off all my do, do, do work tasks, apply essential oils and listen to chill music rather than an action-orientated podcast. It sets up my *feminine energy*, ready to receive and be present for the kids and my husband when he gets home from work.

View conflict as a third party

Conflict is not between *you and him*. It's between *us* and the *conflict*. How do we problem solve as a team? How do we look at conflict as an opponent, not each other as the enemy?

Don't RSVP to every party invite

What's the energy of the dialogue? Is it hostile, tense, competitive, or defensive?

I decline these types of party invitations—I don't engage. Sometimes, the *need-to-be-right* ego takes over. The key is to see it happening in real-time and cue Craig David's, 'I'm walking away' for that moment. Walk away mentally or physically. I'm not suggesting avoiding communication here. I'm simply suggesting he sometimes has off days. We don't need to add fuel to the fire. He wants you to be happy

Are you seeking ways to see this is true, or are you spotting ways where he's letting you down?

As Tony Robbins says, 'Where focus goes, energy flows'.

Attention grows where energy goes. The power of our mind is colossal. Our brains are like search engines. The results you create in your marriage stem directly from what thoughts you enter in the search bar.

> 'We are what we think. All that we are arises with our thought. With our thoughts, we make our world.' - Gautama Buddha

I am responsible for my happiness

It's my job, not his. He can add to it. When we delegate our happiness to someone else, what happens if they have a bad day? Claim your power back. You're in control.

'Anything you can't control in life is teaching you to let go.' – Unknown

The KISS method: 4 steps to connection

We can't control others, but we are in control of our response. That's why I love the word *response-ability*. You can respond. If you're keen to build emotional wealth in your marriage and not sure where to start, use my tools below.

I created *The KISS Method: 4 Steps to Connection*, designed to arm you with simple and practical tools to start implementing right away. Allow one week for each step, and don't rush it. Be present with each step. Remember, you can't microwave your marriage!

Step 1: Know	Step 2: Integrate	Step 3: Audit	Step 4: Solicit
AWARENESS	ALIGN	AUDIT	ASK
Know your love language.	Clean up your mind. Get closer to congruency.	Become a private investigator; seek to understand.	Make a request; ask for what you need.
Know his love language	Align what you say and do.	Ask curious questions. Inquire. Take notes. Clean the slate. Explore in awe.	Requests vs Demands. Note: they are very different.
Know yourself. What are your values? What makes you happy?	Establish boundaries. Say no to say yes.	In what ways are you respecting him?	Use Alison Armstrong's *Ask Formula*.

The KISS method

K – Know each other's love language and know yourself.

The absence of knowing our needs leads to the alternative: expecting he's a mind reader and being disappointed with him for not delivering something he didn't know he was delegated. Email me, and I'll send you a PDF of the *Proust Questionnaire*, which will help you uncover your values.

I – Integrate awareness with actions.

Do you do the things that you say matter? Do you live in unity with your values? For example, your health value is high, yet you find yourself binging on *Netflix* rather than exercising and eating well. Be really honest with yourself. No one is judging here.

Ramit Sethi says, 'Show me your bank statement, and I'll show you your values.' There's nothing wrong with where you spend money. The point is, don't kid yourself. Don't say health is highly valued if you spend lots of money on fast food and alcohol. See the incongruence? Step 2 aligns your values with your actions. Spend more than one week in this step if you have to.

S – Study your interactions and thoughts.

Have child-like curiosity. Why did he say or do that? I wonder what caused him to make that decision. How am I showing up? Am I telling him how to pack the dishwasher? This is the phase to audit your household interactions and conversations. Write down what you notice.

S – Solicit your request.

Ask for what you need. Take note here that there is a difference between a request and a demand. Alison Armstrong has a powerful framework to ask for what you need and get it. You simply state your need. Explain what it looks like with detailed specifics. Share what it will provide for you. And lastly, ask if he needs anything from you to get you what you need.

Nathalie Biviano

Ready to pour self-care into your marriage?

We already know you're into elevating yourself—evidenced by reading a self-help book! You're acutely aware you can't control anyone but yourself, and you take full responsibility for how you show up on your end. That's radical self-responsibility. And that right there is paramount to creating an incredible marriage and life.

Suppose you'd like to sprinkle more self-care into your marriage by deepening conversations. In that case, you can download a free mini e-book I wrote called *5 Powerful Phrases Every Woman Should Master For Connected Conversations*.

Available to download from: linktr.ee/spinetinglingmarriage.

Nathalie Biviano

Nathalie Biviano is a trauma-informed life coach specialising in navigating marriage after babies. She is also a Mama Rising® Facilitator and a matrescence activist. She holds a Bachelor's Degree in Communication, which she discovered was completely useless when she was in the quicksand of marriage conflict and needed real-life communication skills.

Thank God she found mentors and coaching!

At the peak of her corporate career, she realised ordering room service for one was lonely and soulless, and she concluded corporate life was not for her. In 2011, she swapped suits and heels to be a stay-at-home-mama. Fiercely grappling with this new identity and navigating marital conflict, she became dedicated to marriage mastery. After working things out in her own marriage, she coached women whose husbands were 'good men', but their marriage was void of connection, communication, and conflict resolution skills.

Nathalie believes women are the leaders and healers of the home. When they're firm and solid in their values and voice and have powerful self-coaching tools, women self-activate their buried intuition and start living richer lives on their own terms and conditions.

Her mission is to elevate emotional intimacy. When we unburden our lives from emotional heaviness—we set ourselves free.

She lives on the Gold Coast with her favourite humans, Rob, Zara and Massimo. Nathalie is devoted, in awe of her clients, and grateful to live and breathe her dharma daily. Currently, she's working on creating a self-paced program to help even more mamas fall back in love with marriage, motherhood, and themselves.

Connect with Nathalie
IG/FB
@spinetinglingmarriage
www.nathaliebiviano.com
nat@nathaliebiviano.com

Kelly Kilah
Self-Care Reqiures Balance

'The juggle is impossible. It all feels too overwhelming and we begin to feel like a failure.' - Lorraine Murphy

Does this sound like a familiar experience? If this quote resonates with you, you aren't alone. To most mums I share this quote with, it's like a light bulb switches on, and suddenly they feel a wave of relief.

Lorraine continues to explain the unbelievable and unachievable goal of juggling by pointing out that,

> 'The moment a woman births a baby and attempts to then go back to work after having said baby, she is expected overnight to be able to juggle. The worst thing, in my opinion? That we expect ourselves to be able to juggle! So what we have is millions of women setting themselves up every single day in a vain attempt to master a skill that…we cannot master. We can't actually juggle, but we tell ourselves, and society tells us, that we should be able to juggle.'

So what is the alternative to aimlessly juggling, which we know leads to this sense of failure and that we're doing it wrong somehow?

Stop trying to juggle

We need to stop struggling in vain to juggle motherhood, work and our lifestyles in general. If we stop juggling aimlessly, we can discover why we constantly feel like we're failing. We can let the lightbulb go on and learn that this feeling has nothing to do with what we accomplish as mothers.

When my clients have this light bulb moment, I visibly see the relief wash over their faces and their tense shoulders relax. I hope you will feel the same wave of relief wash over you when you've read this chapter.

It took me years to find a better way to avoid the juggle and the inevitable path to feeling like a failure. By sharing my story of breaking through the cycle of self-destruction and exhaustion, I will show you a different technique resulting in an easier and more enjoyable life. My radical approach to motherhood prevents burnout and encourages mums to take control of their own life experiences.

Life before kids

Before children, I was a hard-working and very focused maths, science and Marine Science high school teacher. I loved being single and put all my efforts into my work. I ran activities and school trips after school, on weekends and even on my holidays. I loved what I did and felt like I had an endless supply of energy to devote to these endeavours.

Everything I did in my life was purposeful and directed towards achieving something. I was ambitious and driven. I took a year off work and travelled around the world on my own and loved it.

When I returned home, I decided to move towns and find work in an area of my home state where I've always wanted to live. I was always determined, often called stubborn, which I take as a compliment, and often made decisions and then made them happen.

Navigating Motherhood

Life after kids

It all changed when I became a mother. Admittedly, it wasn't helped by the fact that I had twins for my first pregnancy and again for my last. I released two eggs to have my fraternal boy and girl twins, but multiples run heavily in my husband's family. His father was a triplet, and he has twin sisters, so we were certainly not going back for any further pregnancies.

Within the first four months, I felt I was losing my mind. With hindsight, I now realise this is very typical with newborn multiples, but this was my first motherhood experience. I sought professional advice through my doctor and community health nurses, and thankfully, they determined that I was *just* sleep-deprived, not suffering from postnatal depression.

I still remember the revelation one community health nurse pointed out. After asking what profession I was in, she gave this knowing nod and smile. She told me that it was typical for teachers to suffer when first entering motherhood because of how unpredictable raising children, especially babies, was to how controlled their class environment usually is. This idea made so much sense to me and helped me understand why I was struggling so much.

On the right path

Our first task was sorting the twin's sleep routine, so there was time to think and relax my body and mind. As the twins got older, they continued to fall asleep well at night, self-settling and sleeping through. My daughter slept all night from four months, whereas it took two-and-a-half years for my son. While this made evenings more peaceful, I was too tired from the day to enjoy them. Instead, I often spent the first half hour mindlessly scrolling and procrastinating. I would go to bed, having accomplished very little.

I went through a period of blaming others and circumstances for any unhappiness I felt. Over time, I realised that my happiness was in my control, and I needed to find balance in my life. Instead of putting all my effort into my kids and their lives, I had to create space for myself. If I wanted to achieve true balance, I needed to make time for myself and my needs.

How I achieved balance

I started writing a list of my weekly needs, separated into three categories because it's all about balance. The three categories I used were body, mind and soul, but you could use any words that match your personality. Their purpose is to create a balanced variety of needs simply.

Body	Mind	Soul
Walking	Reading	Beach
Pilates	Mediation	Piano
Nutritious work lunches		Friends
Nutritious snacks		

As I teach my clients, writing this list was only the beginning for me. If I stopped with this simple list of things I wanted to do in life, then nothing would ever change. I'd just feel like a failure for setting these amazing-sounding goals but never managing to achieve them. The secret is to schedule these things to make them happen until they become habits.

I learnt that my needs couldn't be an afterthought when the kids were asleep at night. I had to make myself and my needs a priority with purpose. It was my responsibility to do so to benefit myself and my family.

Reread these last two sentences if you need to. I actually write a 'permission note' for my client's spouse or partner that permits them to make themselves a priority. Honestly, though, we often need to permit ourselves to make us a priority, not everyone else.

I decided to do Pilates between 5.30 and 6am, when my kids usually wake up. It took them some time to get used to me doing this, but they would hang out with me, chatting, reading and playing their own games. It has become quite a bonding time, and I am proud to show my kids that I prioritise my body.

I used to love walking, but I hadn't been as often since the kids migrated out of their double pram. I told myself it was just too hard. Honestly, it hadn't been too hard for a while, but I still wasn't doing it. Now the kids and I will walk somewhere on weekends or school holidays. I mix up the locations to keep it interesting, sometimes the beach, a local bushwalk or down to the nearby park.

One weeknight, I cook two meals. One is for dinner that night, and the other I portion out for my work lunches for next week. Yes, this adds to the fullness of that evening, but the pressure it removes for the following week is so worth it.

Reading novels also disappeared from my life in the early years of raising children. I developed a story I didn't have time for and should have been doing something more constructive that served another purpose for the family. How wrong I was! To get to bed early enough to have reading time, I set the alarm on my phone every night, reminding me it was time to go to bed.

Reading a book before sleeping has many benefits. I'm avoiding screens, so my melatonin levels naturally increase, and my mind starts to wind down for sleep. Focusing on a story means worrying about that day or the next isn't possible. I combine this reading time with lying on my Shakti Mat, resulting in about ten-to-twenty minutes of transition toward a good night's sleep. Priceless!

How you can achieve balance

Self-care isn't about massages or spa treatments for me, although I do partake in these a few times a year and love them. Rather, it's about creating a balanced life you're not constantly wanting a break from. Every day you can add something to help your body, mind and soul so that you rarely, because never say never, feel overwhelmed or overloaded.

Are you ready? If you regularly feel overwhelmed, overloaded and unsupported, it's time to get your life back into balance. What is self-care about for you?

Use the blank table below to add your own needs to balance out your life every day and do it successfully. What do you need to feel balanced, rested and energised? Remember, you can alter the category titles to suit your life.

Body	Mind	Soul

Make the change happen

Once you've added your ideas, it's time to get down to the integrity and commitment part. How and when will you make these things happen? This is the action part that can change your life. Write them down and brainstorm. You can add them to your calendar or on your phone. I recommend writing them down on paper and sticking them on the bathroom mirror, your fridge, or both. Hold integrity for yourself by committing to doing these and then sticking to it.

Unfortunately, if it were as easy as that, you would have already added these things to your life. If you're adding extra things into your life, something that already exists will have to be reduced or removed. What will change so your life is balanced with activities you enjoy? Will you need to get up earlier or go to bed earlier? Will you need to reduce your television time or Facebook scrolling? Are you worth that? Of course you are!

You and your family will benefit when you find a better balance in your life. Everyone will see, experience and appreciate a better version of you. A version where you have more energy, mental space for conversations and life's uncertainties, and more room for flexibility.

Ditch the juggle and enjoy the balance

Once you have started making time and space for your needs, you will notice the difference in yourself immediately. You will feel prioritised, rewarded and important. The coolest part of this process is that no one else is necessarily doing anything for you. You simply made your needs fulfilled. You took control and changed your everyday life for the better. You should be proud of yourself!

I call this process Modern Motherhood Method how to be the best mum in the busy modern world that we live in and the one we create for ourselves.

Kelly Kilah

Kelly is a wife and mother of seven-year-old twins, Emma and Aaron. She lives on the Sunshine Coast in Queensland, Australia. Her mission is to prevent many of the silent mental health issues that mums face in this modern world of parenting. Kelly works with mums of newborns through to teenagers, helping them enjoy their motherhood journey and raise healthy, resilient children.

Kelly is an established Self-Care Coach who has been working with mums for decades to help them successfully navigate the challenging phases of motherhood, sleeping, feeding, behaviour and anything connected with mothering while learning to reconnect with themselves.

Through group and one-on-one coaching, Kelly guides women through simple strategies that help them restore the balance between being a woman, a mum, a partner and everything else we are trying to be to everyone around us. The women Kelly works with ultimately feel like they've found themselves again and spend time on themselves unselfishly. By reconnecting with self, the motherhood journey is easier and filled with more joy, which trickles into all aspects of life.

Kelly developed the Modern Motherhood Method, which she sees as preventative care in the mental health space, particularly among professional women who struggle with the unpredictable nature of children, just as she did herself.

How to work with Kelly

Kelly has programs and courses to suit all stages of motherhood, from newborns to toddlers to teenagers and beyond. Her focus is on making your life easier and more enjoyable, which has a flow-on effect for the rest of your family. Kelly offers free membership in her Facebook Group called Getting Back to Your Essentials and has a four-month signature program called Change My Life Mastermind Program which only opens twice a year.

Get in touch with her to see how she can help you!
Website: www.essentialsonly.com.au
Facebook: https://www.facebook.com/essentialsonly.kelly
Instagram: https://www.instagram.com/essentialsonly.kelly
Email: info@essentialsonly.com.au

Leticia Corrina
The Energetic Shift

'Your baby wouldn't survive without a strong adult connection. If that adult is thriving, they'll thrive too.' - Leticia Corrina

I went from thinking I couldn't do my normal 'pre-baby practises' to look after my mental health to realising my baby loved being a part of it. I discovered it is possible to do dancing breathwork with a baby in the morning and mini meditations all day long!

If you take your mind back to your pre-baby days, you had all the time in the world to do whatever you liked, right? Of course, you had your life, family and work obligations, but if you decided you needed some time to yourself or wanted to have time each morning to set your day up, you could. I spent the first few hours setting the frequency for the day, drinking cacao, a heart-opening medicine, dancing, meditating, reading and doing yoga.

Boy, I struggled as I stepped into motherhood and committed every waking second to ensuring this tiny new human would survive! Setting my mornings up the way I used to was a thing of the past—or so I thought!

Spending hours each day getting my mindset right seems crazy, but luckily, halfway through my self-employed journey for the last decade, I realised my mindset was the most important marker for my success. If I set my mindset up correctly, I could better navigate the world around me. I would also shorten or lengthen my morning routine based on my available time.

I realised I was really struggling when I was three months postpartum. Of course, the extreme sleep deprivation didn't help, but neither did my total lack of self-care. The term *self-care* is colonised and commercialised, but it was coined in the 1950s by civil rights activists, and it meant *self-care as a radical act of self-preservation*. So not all bubble baths, wine and girls' nights like in the movies. Not just all the nice fluffy stuff but actually a radical act to commit to putting yourself first—we all know you can't pour from an empty cup.

For me, I so needed my mornings back.

I realised that I wouldn't be able to meditate with a busy bubba on the go, so I had to figure out how to break down my old self-care routine into mini mum moments for myself with my baby girl.

What this meant was I slowed things down even more! My old routine to *set the frequency* by drinking cacao and getting into dancing turned into twenty minutes of slowly drinking and setting the room up, so it was fun for the baby. I'd place her toys around, make lots of eye contact, and smile rather than close my eyes and look inward. I'd choose new music for my dancing meditation, which we both liked. I have to say that my pre-baby music was far more intense than I have now.

Many of you may never have danced for mediation, so let me explain. Of course, you can just do it any way you like, but below I will outline how I activate different parts of my body, soul, and mind to get set up for the day.

If this interests you, join me

Leticia Corrina

Work with the elements
Earth, water, fire, air and ether

- To earth, I jump around and stamp the ground. I anchor my feet and ball my hands into fists after a while.
- Softly I tap my lower back to activate my kidneys.
- My hands move to my shoulders, then tap the top of my head, around my face, collarbones and down my front. I'll wake my legs and my arms.
- I repeat this three times or as long as one song lasts.

I feel grounded, strong, present and awake.

- Next, I sit in Lotus Pose or as close as my achy body lets me that day, and I start to swirl my body around in slow, small circles.
- The circles get bigger until my whole body swirls forwards and backwards.
- I'll repeat this one way, then the other, for as long as a song.

I feel fluid and free, like beautiful-running water.

- Now, *The breath of fire* or, as I like to call it, *the ego-annihilator*. It takes all of your focus and strength to do this for a few rounds and your ego really tries to stop you. But when you push through and successfully finish your sets, your whole body feels lighter and refreshed.
- Stay sitting in Lotus Pose, raise your arms above your head with clenched fists, close your eyes and your mouth and picture yourself getting punched in the stomach—crazy, I know! Your stomach should jump inwards, and your breath should be forced out of

your nose. Repeat this movement and force *out* breath every second for thirty to sixty seconds. On the final *out-breath*, hold for as long as possible before taking a huge breath in through your nose, then exhale and relax.
- Shake your body and arms around and repeat another two to three times when you're ready.
- Choose a shorter, faster song to help keep you in time.

This is also used therapeutically to help people release negative energy stored deep in their cellular memory and is great to do at any time of the day to re-centre.

*Not to be practised while pregnant

I feel fired-up, radiant and ready to go.

Air to open your heart space

- In Lotus Pose, breathe in slowly, lean your head back and open your arms out.
- Exhale and drop your head, rounding your back and pushing your arms forward.
- Envision bringing all the love into your body as you breathe in, lean back with open arms, and then push any last negative thoughts, feelings, or stuck memories you don't feel good about out and away as you exhale.
- Repeat this slow inhale and exhale, sweeping your arms in and out a few times and then bringing your hands to the ground.

Time to breathe the love in and blow any last negativity away.

- Ether is the element that connects us to spirit and intuition. So, with your hands on the ground, close your eyes and tune in to *Pachamama*, Mother Earth. Envision an energy cord from your belly button to the earth's core. Feel the energy from *Her* come back, strong and safe, back to you, holding you with *Her* love, just as we do our babies.

- Sweep your arms above your head and thank our Heavenly Father, the Universe, God or whatever you believe in for always being there, constant, strong and supportive.

To me, *He* represents the healthy masculine, *our* healthy inner masculine. Where all of us are seen, and all of us are perfect in our imperfections. It took me years to get to this place. So stay strong in your healthy, supportive routines, and I hope you find the inner-masculine strength that can hold you through anything too.

Imagine a protective ball of energy around you, picture negativity or judgement coming at you and see it hit your protective energy ball and bounce back as love. Remember that this exists during your day, especially during rough moments.

Stretch your arms out wide, then engulf yourself in a tight hug while saying, 'Thank you, thank you, thank you,' repeatedly. Give yourself the love and peace you desire first, and then bring that into your day.

From this space, I feel tuned in and deeply supported during my day.

I completely understand if you are utterly confused right now! You can access links to videos in my bio to help you along.

It's quite an intense and powerful morning ritual, and after doing it daily for four years straight, the first three months of motherhood knocked me. But, the thing with kids I've found is that they *love* just being around you, especially when you make silly faces, dance like a crazy person and have fun with them.

Navigating Motherhood

Once I adapted to drinking the heart-opening cacao with my girl, she *loved* me dancing around. She watched me swirl close to her and far away, taking *crazy* big breaths in her face and engulfing her in hugs as I opened my heart. She watched until she was old enough to join in or just play with whatever toys were around if she lost interest.

Pure Cacao is amazing in this process.

Pure Cacao is an earlier stage of chocolate, and yes, our draw to chocolate is a true-natural draw, and the darker it is, the more cacao is in there. But not all chocolate is equal.

It's often called *Ceremonial Cacao* or *100% Cacao Paste*. This means it contains the whole cacao bean and is cared for at every stage, including the farmers who grow it. The Master Grower is a mama just like us and gets what it is to be a mama. I call her *Mama Cacao*.

Ceremonial Cacao is about Awakening. Mama Cacao supports the heart, connects us to our inner essence, opens us to our higher self, supports courage to take our next steps in life, opens pathways to positivity and joy and supports mindfulness.

The medicine in her Cacao helps our bodies with high levels of antioxidants, magnesium and iron and our mind with chemicals that provide uplifting and mental clarity. I brew a *cuppa* with a little sweetener and drink her slowly with intention while asking for support. Again, there is information in my bio to see how I make it and what I use.

For me, it was simply a mindset shift from needing things to being specific ways to finding a way to bring in my daughter's joy as she started her days like this too. And to finish off, usually, I meditate, lying on the floor, eyes closed, hands and feet outstretched, for as long as I feel I need to.

I found this to be damn dull for my girl, and the only part I got a little frustrated in was if I was distracted, which I mean, of course, I was because I had my beautiful baby girl to keep safe.

So I wasn't going to be closing my eyes to go inwards for ten-plus minutes.

Breastfeeding became my meditation

One of my close friends has an early childhood education centre and is very well versed in child psychology, so I listened closely to her while pregnant. She'd mentioned how she disliked seeing women breastfeeding and on their phones because it disconnected from the primal needs they were providing. I remember paying particular attention when she said this because it felt so true to me. So I decided that I would always be present while feeding.

Fast forward to the first latch my midwife helped me with and the joy of those first few days. We captured so many moments with my camera, which I am glad we did, but it meant my phone wasn't away while feeding as intended. I need to say I'm so lucky and grateful that I'm able to breastfeed and enjoy it. I understand this is not the case for everyone, but this beautiful pocket of time happens no matter if bubs is breastfed or snuggled close with a bottle. Either way is perfect for you and your baby. All that matters is that you are *present* for whatever method it takes to feed. This is a pocket of time where the baby is relaxed, and you can't move or do anything else. So why not choose to meditate and be still rather than scroll like a zombie on social media?

It was really hard to stick to at first, but once I committed, it only took me one week to truly feel the difference. After the first few days, I resisted less. I'd turn my phone on flight mode whenever bub was due to feed. I tried to ensure we were always in our feeding chair. I created a special space for us to be.

After a week, I realised because I was so focused on being focused on feeding that, this was, in fact, exactly like meditating. I used to focus on one thing or nothing, which cleared my mind and let in the space to work through what I needed. Suddenly, every two hours, because bub likes to feed a lot, I had the chance to be still, clear my mind and let myself feel again.

I wanted to share a chapter in this incredible book to help other mothers see it's possible to keep space for themselves and show that it can also be a beautiful bonding time with your child. I wanted to help mothers disconnect from all the noise around them and reconnect with the innate knowledge we all have to mother our children.

The step into motherhood was the most difficult step I've taken in my life. If you want to make your at-home alone feeding time a chance to tune in and reconnect with yourself, I'll share the things that worked for me.

Key things to help with connection

Set up a beautiful feeding space with a comfy chair, and pop your phone into flight mode. Choose a few songs that help you stay present each time you feed.

If I was feeding before sleep, I loved to play the last three songs in 'Songs for Bubbas' by Anika Moa, or if it was one of the day feeds, then my favourite was 'I Release Control' by Alexa Sunshine Rose and 'The Power Is Here Now' by Alexia Chellun.

Once we were set up to feed, I would envisage that same energy cord mentioned from my morning practice above, but this time one from my belly button and one from my daughters, with both of us connecting deep into Mother Earth. I would ask for support and peace and picture that protective energy bubble of white light surrounding us both.

After the songs are finished, I take ten deep breaths in through my nose, out through my mouth and then hold for ten seconds. I repeat for twenty breaths and a twenty-second hold, and then finally, thirty breaths and a hold for as long as I can manage.

If she was fighting sleep, I would start again once she calmed down. This would keep me calm also.

While it may seem impossible to have meditation time with a bubba

Leticia Corrina

now, finding these little pockets of time throughout your day may just work wonders for your mental health. It's nice to realise I'm feeding my mind while nourishing my wee one.

I only have one baby. However, I have heard that you can create a special little toy box for your toddler or toddlers that they're only allowed to play with while you're feeding. I look forward to trying this out one day in the future!

This energetic shift is available to you, too. Your baby wouldn't survive without you. If you're thriving, they'll thrive too.

I'm available online through my *Instagram* to help you with this shift. So please do come and say hi!

Leticia Corrina

Leticia Corrina has been a serial entrepreneur for over a decade. She has built huge communities in the health and wellness space and is passionate about showing people what living an inspired life and bringing visions to reality can look like for them. After travelling the world on and off for over ten years, Leticia rushed home to New Zealand when the pandemic hit to be near her family. While home, Leticia rekindled love, and they were blessed to welcome their miracle child in 2021. The whirlwind time that followed made Leticiastrip everything back to basics while she navigated this new stage of life. Now she's passionate about helping other mums remember who they are and the importance of making time for themselves amongst the chaos.

If you want to connect with Leticia, see video explanations of her morning dance meditation and cacao making or access any playlists she uses, head over to her Instagram account.

Connect with Leticia
Instagram: @leticiacorrina

Kate Hamilton
Perfection – You've Already Achieved It

'I always find beauty in things that are odd and imperfect— they are much more interesting.' - Marc Jacobs

Welcome to my story of how the birth of an amazing-beautiful boy threw his mother into the wonderful world of special needs parenting and helped change her unhealthy relationship with perfectionism.

Perfectionism is such an interesting concept, isn't it? While many people believe there is nothing wrong with aiming for perfection, the reality of true perfection is non-existent. Unfortunately, many strive for some form of false perfection, failing to notice the real perfection taking place around them. It's taken me a while to understand, but I'm a confessed perfectionist. I'm not a perfectionist who never has a hair out of place or who manages to decorate their house perfectly and has zero specks of dirt, after all, I have three kids, but I'm what I refer to as a big-picture perfectionist. Ideally, I'd like to live my life exactly how I plan and envision it.

Certain traits feed my perfectionism. I call them the Evil P's—planning, people pleasing, I particularly hate this one, and often a lack of patience. Using the word 'evil' may sound melodramatic, but these traits cause me to put myself last, pressure my family and me to achieve the impossible, avoid confrontation and not stand up for myself. They cause me to allow others to walk all over me. In my opinion, anything that stops you from living your best life is a form of evil. Not the best life planned in your mind or what you see on social media, but your actual best life. Does any of this sound familiar? I know I am not the only woman, or person for that matter, who relates to struggling with one or all the Evil P's.

I unconsciously struggled with the Evil P's well into my thirties until something quite unbelievable happened. The arrival of my second child didn't go at all according to my perfect plan, but despite the heartache and traumatic events that ensued, my son enabled me to recognise my unhealthy relationship with the Evil P's. He gave me such incredible clarity and introduced me to the amazing world of special needs parenting. A world filled with hundreds of inspiring stories, strong-beautiful children and their parents, and a place where you learn what true perfection really is.

The perfect life

I can't really pinpoint where or why my perfectionism began. I'm sure, like many things, my childhood and upbringing contributed. I grew up in a relatively small district where everyone knew everyone's business. It felt like all your flaws and mistakes were displayed for everyone to see, judge and comment on. Or perhaps something in that second X chromosome causes females to be meticulous-little planners. What drives the need to have everything organised and sorted, not allowing for mistakes, heartache or flaws? Or is it just simply me? I'll never know what caused me to want everything to look and be perfect or be such an unbelievable people pleaser, but it was something I continued to do, and I brought it with me into my motherhood journey.

Being a mother has been something I wanted for as long as I can remember, from playing mothers and fathers in primary school to picking out baby names and designing their nurseries. Motherhood was always on the cards, but it took until my thirties to get there. Then finally, I met and married my soulmate, and a few months after the wedding, I was pregnant with our first child.

Being the planner I am, I discovered as early as possible that we were having a baby girl. After a perfect pregnancy and a slightly less-than-perfect but relatively drama-free delivery, my husband and I welcomed our beautiful baby girl, Alexandra Ellis. She couldn't have been more perfect if I'd planned her. She popped out looking divine, fed amazingly well, and slept…well, good enough for a newborn. Alexandra was everything a new mother could hope for. Every milestone was met early, and looked beautiful doing it. I was the smug new mum, and Alexandra was the ideal child to continue to feed my perfectionism. Time for another. I mean, why wouldn't we do this all over again? Time for a perfect sibling to go with my perfect daughter to continue my well-planned perfect life that people are pleased about!

A spanner in the works

The second time around didn't go as easily or perfectly as I thought it would. We had trouble conceiving and sadly suffered a miscarriage. But after a bit of difficulty, I was finally pregnant again and was fairly convinced our bad luck was behind us. However, I had some very uneasy feelings, even at this early stage, but I put it down to the miscarriage. I did everything I could to ensure this baby was going to be okay, including all the prenatal testing.

After getting the all-clear from the tests and finding out this baby was a boy, my planning and perfectionist ways kicked back into gear. Perfect! A pigeon pair, exactly how I wanted it. I completely expected my baby boy would be the male version of my daughter, and everything was going to be just so completely perfect. I think back to this time now and laugh about how naïve and deluded I was about so many things.

This pregnancy was nowhere near as enjoyable as my first, but I got through the nine months, and we finally welcomed our baby boy, Mason John Robert. However, this is where things unravelled a little for me. When Alex was born, she popped out bright-eyed, bushy-tailed, looking just beautiful. Mason, on the other hand, came out covered in vernix. He took a long time to open his eyes properly, and well, let's just say he sort of had a face that only a mother could love. At this point, I had to tell myself to stop comparing him to Alex. So, as we progressed, things were, well…fine. Mason was feeding well and sleeping, and everything seemed good, not perfect, but okay. However, I couldn't shake that uneasy feeling. I was definitely having some trouble fitting him into my perfect life, but it was also more than that. My mother's instinct told me that maybe there could be more than perfectionism at play here.

By the time Mason was four months old, it was clear something wasn't right. He was sleeping all day, still had poor head control, and showed no signs of wanting to roll or being able to grasp or track objects. All things that Alexandra was well and truly mastering at this point. I continued to visit our doctors, and I could tell they could see some red flags, but there wasn't enough to say, 'Yes, I think something could be wrong here'.

People continued to remind me not to compare him to his sister, the perfect one, and that he would do things in his own time. But as we edged closer to the five-month mark and there was still no progress, we decided to take him to the paediatrician just to ensure everything was ok. My instincts as a mother were screaming that it was time to act. So, after a trip to the paediatrician, a few tests, a hospital visit and genetic testing, we were finally delivered the news that no amount of planning can ever prepare you. Not only was there a problem with our precious baby boy, but there was a massive life-altering problem.

Mason was diagnosed with a very rare condition called Allan-Herndon Dudley Syndrome, also known as MCT8 deficiency.

MCT8 is a protein responsible for transporting thyroid hormones into the brain. These thyroid hormones are critical for brain development.

As these hormones can't get to the brain, patients suffer from serious cognition, motor development and general health delays. It is often misdiagnosed because it presents similarly to cerebral palsy. It primarily affects males, although a very small amount females are diagnosed. It's extremely rare. In the last official count, there were 320 people diagnosed worldwide. However, now the numbers hover closer to 400. The chance of this happening is roughly one in fifty-four million. That number is one of the reasons we call Mason our little unicorn.

My husband and I were delivered one of our worst nightmares at that moment. From then on, we were thrown into the world of special parenting.

One afternoon, I finally gave in and went into deep research mode. I was confronted with images and descriptions of serious disabilities. It knocked the wind out of me so hard I don't know how I ever got up again. I just sat on the couch looking at my future with my baby boy in my arms, and I just cried and cried. This was not the perfect-looking future I had planned. I couldn't believe it. Mason was the last piece of my perfect life puzzle, and I was shattered that it had turned out this way. For the first time in a long time, I felt completely out of control and out of my depth and wasn't too sure what to do. But I did the only thing I knew to do, fight! So, we dived headfirst into the world of special needs parenting, and although we knew what we were dealing with was huge, we also knew there was no option but to do everything we could to help this precious boy live his best possible life. So, that's what we did and continue to do.

Learning True perfectionism

Having a child that doesn't fit into the normal box, let alone a perfect one, stops you in your tracks. I have a child that will never meet typical milestones. He won't ever walk or talk like a neurotypical child. At the beginning of our journey, which is often a stage of denial, nothing was more important to me than working as hard as we could to get Mason to achieve all these milestones as close to what was neurotypically possible. But over time, we are learning that he will achieve things in his own way and on his own timeline. He has introduced us to such a different way of life, a life that makes living the life I originally planned and deemed perfect seem kind of dumb.

Mason gifted me a life-changing perspective on what's important and what is not, and if that wasn't enough, he has gifted me with some bravery. The kind of bravery that allows me to stop caring about what people think and stand up for myself. I finally knew that something looking one hundred per cent perfect isn't real and that mistakes, sweat, grit, and reality are what make something interesting and beautiful.

When I hang pictures in my house now, I never worry if they are straight because that's not what makes them beautiful or inspirational to look at. The message, the people in those pictures and the stories behind them make them perfect to me. Mason also saved me from modelling this behaviour to my daughters. Yes, daughters, we went back for a third, but that's a story for another time. These things my son has gifted me are the greatest gifts I could ever hope to receive. By sharing my story, I hope I can help other Evil P sufferers to stop and think about what is really important. I hope I can help them be confident and brave enough to happily live and embrace their life, warts and all.

But my job here isn't done..

Becoming an advocate

Mason is the bravest, most beautiful boy. He has to endure so much, but he is still the happiest-little soul whose smile lights up the darkest of rooms. He has given me so much, more than I can ever give him. However, my job as his mother, carer and advocate means fighting for change.

Australia has come a long way regarding disability and inclusion, but there is still a way to go. Genetics, birth trauma, health issues and disability do not discriminate. My story could easily be yours, your child's or even your grandchild's. You will face many challenges if you find yourself or a loved one raising a child with a rare disease or disability.

There are so many things that we can do better, and we have a tough job ahead of us in making changes. We fight to receive funding and services like daycares and schools our children can attend. Often there aren't places to change our children in a dignified way that doesn't include squeezing them onto a changing table, using the back of the car, or, when you're truly desperate, a dirty floor. The logistics alone of trying to take our children on outings is daunting, and when you manage it, you feel anxious because people stare or they are too uncomfortable to interact. The most heartbreaking is realising that because your child doesn't fit the 'normal' box, they don't belong, or it's too much effort to include them.

I don't quite know where to start, but I am committed to doing whatever I can to contribute to this change. We will continue to share our story as it unfolds to help spread awareness and ignite change for those living with rare diseases and disabilities in our community, country and even the world.

There is a well-known quote by Amy Wright, a mother of two children with Down Syndrome, that many of us in the special needs community know. It goes, 'I wouldn't change you for the world, but I'll change the world for you.' And so that's just what I'll do…

Kate Hamilton

Kate Hamilton is a trained early childhood teacher who continues to pursue her love of teaching.

Along with teaching and being a mother, Kate is now very passionate about continuing to share her story of raising a child with a rare disease. Through writing her blog and social media pages, she hopes to continue raising awareness for disability and rare diseases.

Kate hopes to continue contributing to help raise funds for the MCT8 Foundation in the hopes that one day a cure can be found for MCT8 deficiency.

Kate hopes that her work, determination, and love for her son will help her find ways to improve accessibility, public understanding, and inclusion and encourage conversations around disability and what it's like for people and families living with rare diseases in Australia.

Kate is passionate about creating a more inclusive world because everybody has the right to be included and experience everything the world has to offer.

To learn more, you can follow Kate and her family on their journey.

Kate Hamilton

Website: www.masemansmum.com.au
Facebook: Mase.Mans.Mum | Facebook
Instagram: @mase.mans.mum

Amy Campbell
Imposter Syndrome

'Fake it till you make it.' - English aphorism

Have you ever felt you're faking it till you make it? Yeah, me too. This idiom was my survival tool in life, but I feel like this mentality gave me imposter syndrome. Imposter syndrome is defined In the Macquarie Dictionary as a '...state of mind in which an individual, although high-achieving, nevertheless feels that their achievements are a mistake or a piece of luck, and that they will be found out at any moment for being worthless and incompetent.'

Difficulty accepting my accomplishments is me all over, in all I do in life. I always feel like the praise I get is undeserving. This isn't just in motherhood but across the board. For example, I've worked in the beauty industry as a celebrity spray tanner, tanning some of the biggest names in Australia. I've been named the preferred spray tanner to the stars for the *TV Week Logie Awards* five years in a row. I've opened an award-winning salon in Sydney that employs over fourteen staff and has almost 10,000 clients on the books. Yet, I still feel that it's difficult to accept praise for my accomplishments because of imposter syndrome. More recently, I felt the imposter syndrome deeply on my motherhood journey.

Amy Campbell

I struggled with fertility for over five years, trying to conceive through in-vitro fertilisation (IVF) due to stage four endometriosis, resulting in blocked tubes and no chance of natural conception. I was diagnosed at just fifteen and had my first laparoscopy surgery at nineteen when the devastating news natural conception wasn't an option. Being told that news at such a young age was a lot take on board. Lucky for me, my mum was an endometriosis sufferer, and so was my sister, so I had plenty of support around me. My sister did IVF for many years, so I knew the process and was well aware of what I was in for. Or was I?

In 2014, my husband and I started our IVF journey after being married for eighteen months. We ventured into this fertility world alone, thinking it would work the first time. Unfortunately, it didn't, and I struggled in silence behind closed doors for the first two years before I decided it was time to open up. I wanted to remove the taboos around the subject, so I started documenting my journey on my social media platform as if it were a normal part of life. After five years and eight IVF attempts, ectopic pregnancy in 2017, which led to emergency surgery and the removal of both fallopian tubes, followed by a miscarriage in 2018, I finally conceived my daughter, Alinta Jean, in November 2019. The fertility journey was tough, and pregnancy at thirty-eight was also tough. Then I thought motherhood would be a walk in the park because we are born to do this, right? Boy was I wrong.

Alinta's birth was traumatic. She was born unresponsive and needed resuscitation on a table behind a curtain next to me. Thankfully, Alinta pulled through and was absolutely perfect! Sadly, my vagina was a casualty of this traumatic event. I suffered a prolapse bladder and bowel, something I knew nothing about, but I knew something was very wrong. My Pelvic Floor Physiotherapist confirmed my prolapses at six weeks postpartum.

My rehabilitation was very long, and I still suffer today. As if that wasn't bad enough, I struggled to breastfeed. It just didn't come naturally to me.

Navigating Motherhood

My daughter was losing weight and not getting enough milk. I got up every two hours during the night and pumped to get milk out of my breasts on the lounge for hours. I ate my body weight in Boobie Cookies daily, trying to help produce more breast milk. Doing that made me gain weight, so there went my bounce-back body. I felt so much pressure to achieve.

I was struggling big time. For eight long weeks, I continued this vicious cycle, punishing myself to do what my body was designed to do. I constantly read the amazing comments on my Instagram, and I just felt like an imposter.

The constant messages reassuring me I was doing a great job '…you're doing amazing, Amy…you look fabulous…you're such a natural at this…you're killing it, Mumma.'

But was I? Did people really think I was a great mum and doing great when I could barely get her here safely and now can't even produce enough milk to feed her? I felt like a fraud.

I struggled to conceive, and then with what we are taught our bodies are made for—deliver a baby vaginally and breastfeed. Two things I felt I failed. Two things I struggled with so badly. Two things I almost let define me. I soon learnt I was not alone. Many others felt the same feelings. So why was no one talking about these struggles? Why was no one sharing their birth traumas publicly? Was it because we felt ashamed? Once again, I took to social media to share my struggles and the trauma I had experienced.

What did I learn in these early days? I learnt pretty quickly that many people don't talk about the struggles during motherhood. Much like fertility, many women suffer alone and don't speak up. I realised how unhealthy it was to punish myself for doing what I thought I had to do when the reality was a fed baby was a happy baby. I wasn't a failure for switching to formula.

I also learnt that no longer killing myself all night on the lounge trying to pump milk would make me a happier mum. I became the kind of mum that enjoys time with her newborn instead of stressing about having enough breast milk for the next feed. I soon learnt I was not the only one who suffered a traumatic birth, and prolapse and pessaries were a common part of life. But yet again, not many people spoke about this, and I wanted to make sure my journey made other women feel more normal and less alone.

After switching to formula, I soon regained my life, and Alinta thrived—gaining weight weekly and hitting milestones. I felt more like me. I returned to the gym and started doing the daily activities I loved without the stress of that next feed. I also learnt that I was not an imposter. In fact, I was probably more the norm. The person I thought I had to be wasn't the rule. I quickly learnt what imposter syndrome was and that I had put this label on myself in all aspects of my life. It was time to value my worth and ensure I soaked up the praise because I was doing a bloody good job! I should be rewarding myself, not putting myself down.

As a salon owner, I advocate for the importance of self-care and taking time out for yourself, especially for mums. I have watched many mums lose themselves over the past two decades once they have a child. They spend all their time nurturing their children and forgetting to look after themselves. So I knew it was important, once I got past those initial weeks, to get back into the salon and start treating myself to my weekly blow dries and facials and the things that fill my cup so that I could be the best mum for my newborn.

Sometimes it's hard to put ourselves first and allocate time for self-care when we have these gorgeous little humans demanding one hundred per cent of our time and a long list of more important things we think we should be doing.

> 'I believe allocating time to ourselves to do the things that make us feel good will make those other important things feel less tedious and we will feel much less resentment doing them.' - Amy Campbell

I bet you can't even count on one hand the things you do for yourself in a week. But I'm positive the list of things you do for your partner and children is endless. We don't even bat an eyelid at the driving and drop-offs, grocery store pick-ups, cooking and baking, cleaning, ironing, kids' sports and after-school activities. Yet, even on the busiest days, time for all these things is somehow just found. So isn't it time you start finding time on busy days for yourself?

My self-care tips to help fill your cup

Don't be afraid to ask for help. It seems simple, right? If we try to do everything ourselves, we will burn out sooner. Ask for help when you need a time-out.

Allocate a day each week for one hour of you time. This could be just to wash your hair and do a home facial, read a book, or listen to a podcast while drinking a hot cup of coffee, uninterrupted. Get your partner or a friend to look after your baby at the same time every week, so you know that's your 'you' time, and you have something to look forward to.

It sounds simple, but many new mums put themselves last, getting everyone else ready for the day. Sometimes it's after lunch, and they are still un-showered, in pyjamas, and haven't eaten breakfast. So I get up, shower and eat breaky, so I'm ready for the day before my husband goes to work.

Treat yourself to something you love. Whether it's the hairdressers, beauty salons, yoga or dance class, or even just a coffee with a childfree girlfriend, if this makes you feel good, don't feel guilty. Get a babysitter and allocate time, whether it's monthly or weekly. You will feel better for it and be a happier mum if your cup is always full. Remember, you can't pour from an empty cup.

Find social media accounts to follow that make you feel good. Do the accounts you follow align with your values? Are the people you follow authentic and transparent? Or are they just showing you their highlights

Amy Campbell

reel? If you aimlessly scroll through perfectly curated accounts that make you feel bad about yourself, it's time to unfollow and find new inspiration to make you feel more aligned and connected.

My mission over the past two decades was always to make women look and feel their best, so they can live their happiest lives. As a new mum, I know the importance of this when so much more exposure on social media makes many mums feel inferior and less worthy due to the daily content in our feeds.

My Instagram is a safe space for women to reach out to me anytime for a chat, a vent, or ask questions, whether it's about fertility, IVF, endometriosis, toddler drama, pregnancy-related or even beauty tips. This space has no limits, and I love taking time each day to connect with my followers on a real and organic level.

You can follow my journey and reach out to me anytime via my Instagram www.instagram.com/amy_maree_c.

I would love to connect with other like-minded women and share our authentic and raw stories of survival. I am working on my first solo book, which will be released in 2022, and you can find the details on my Instagram as they become available.

I decided to put pen to paper and put all my life experiences and my journey into a book to help others feel less alone, as well as a glimpse into the IVF world and educate people who may have never experienced Infertility. The world now sees one-in-eight couples struggling to conceive and one-in-four pregnancies ending in miscarriage. I believe these topics need to be brought to light, whether it's a part of your journey or not. Let's learn how to support others in these trying times, so people no longer feel ashamed to share their journeys.

Amy Campbell

Amy is one of Sydney's most renowned IVF advocates after battling with endometriosis for two decades before five year battle with IVF, including six stimulated cycles and eight transfers, ectopic pregnancy and miscarriage, before becoming a mum to her double rainbow baby, Alinta Jean, at aged thirty-eight in 2019.

It wasn't always fertility talk with Amy. She was first known for her successful beauty business in Southern Sydney's Sutherland Shire and has a long list of celebrity clients for her sought-after spray tans. Amy's beauty business has always been her passion. She loves to make women feel beautiful inside and out and not feel guilty for looking after themselves. Amy's passion for self-care and squashing the claim that beauty equals vanity is what drove her to run her business for the past two decades and try to change people's mindsets about looking after themselves.

In recent years, once speaking out about her IVF journey and pregnancy loss, her online following began to grow. Keeping her audience engaged and her content real and raw, Amy shares stories about her experiences with endometriosis, IVF, ectopic pregnancy and pregnancy loss,

Amy Campbell

birth trauma, prolapse and postpartum recovery, De Quervain Tendinitis, pregnancy and IVF for baby number two at forty-years-old.

Amy uses her online presence to vocalise what many women go through, but not many feel confident to speak up about it.

Amy's beauty salon is called The Bridal Bar and services everyone for any occasion, giving that special treatment to a bride. Her business runs an annual campaign called, Sorry no more, which asks women to strip down and be confident in their skin and stop apologising for their appearance.

> You can connect with Amy:
> www.amymaree.com.au
> www.bridalbar.com.au
> amy@bridalbar.com.au
> Instagram: www.instagram.com./amy_maree_c
> Facebook: www.facebook.com/amymaree

Lisa Smith
Preparing For Parenthood

'Everyone is running their own race in life, so be empathetic, don't judge and choose kindness' – Lisa Smith

Life is hard. Am I right? We are born as dependents, then become independent and may have dependents. We live to work or work to live, and then we die. I know this sounds morbid, but since having my daughter, Josie, I feel I see life differently now.

When Josie was seven months old, my husband, Brendan, was diagnosed with Postnatal Depression (PND). An article written by Margaret Jawraski states, 'Around 1 in 10 men experience paternal postpartum depression (PPD) after the birth of a child.'

However, since Brendan's diagnosis, many people I speak to, even colleagues who are mental health professionals, were unaware that men or other partners in a same-sex relationship could suffer from PND.

A little bit about me

With consent from my husband, I want to share our story and provide strategies and a step-by-step guide in recognising, validating, and supporting your partner if you believe they are suffering from PND.

Lisa Smith

Let me take a few steps back and introduce myself. I was born and raised in Brisbane, Australia, on 4 October 1989. My parents are still happily married after forty years. I have an older sister, Kate, and a younger brother, Mitchell. I was raised in a comfortable setting and offered every opportunity under the sun—the best education, sport, speech and drama, overseas holidays, and so on.

For these opportunities, I will be forever grateful to my parents. At the time, though, I didn't appreciate it. I struggled academically, which we discovered later in my life was potentially due to a scar on the hippocampus. The hippocampus is responsible for consolidating information from short-term memory to long-term memory. The scar came from bacterial meningitis, which I contracted at twenty months. I remember the day my dad gave me the option to leave school in grade ten and pursue an apprenticeship in hairdressing. Nothing at *all* against hairdressers, but at that moment, I realised maybe, after all the extra private tutoring and support from my school, my parents had given up on me. I decided to finish school and go to university.

So, I worked hard and finished my final year with average grades. I remember thinking how much I wanted to be a nurse at school. However, I was told that nursing wasn't an option because I hadn't completed any science subjects. Instead, I was encouraged to apply for primary school teaching. I was accepted, and my family were proud. However, two years into the degree, I made my first adult decision and transferred and study for a Bachelor of Psychological Science. I finished my degree and completed a Masters in Rehabilitation Counselling.

One lesson from my story so far is that you can do anything if you put your mind to it. Looking back and reflecting on your life so far, what is one piece of advice you'd give someone younger than you?

I worked in an occupational rehabilitation role for a few years, but I still had that voice in the back of my head telling me to become a nurse, but not any type of nurse, a mental health nurse. So, with my husband's support, I quit my job as a rehabilitation consultant and started on a new journey of full-time nursing study.

I completed the degree in two years and graduated with distinction. I was finally a nurse! I was lucky enough to secure a job at the Queensland Children's Hospital (QCH) in the Child Mental Health Inpatient ward, which I found fascinating and challenging but also very rewarding.

My interest in mental health and illness started at a young age. I was always a very open-minded, non-judgemental and empathetic individual. My husband, Brendan, who I met when I was nineteen, twelve years ago, has always said my kindness and caring for other people is what he loves most about me.

When we met, Brendan was emotionally constipated. To this day, our fights revolve around me not knowing how he *truly* feels about me or anything really. So, over time I worked my magic. I provided him with a safe environment where he could share his feelings. Open communication has saved us and helped us continue our relationship for this long.

Yes, like everyone, we've had our ups and downs, and it is not always rainbows and butterflies, but he is home to me. He provides me with security and undeniable love. Over the years, he has learnt to share his feelings with others, even if it means I must give him space in his 'man cave brain' to think about how he'd like to respond to a particular discussion or argument. Not always easy, ladies and gentlemen, but effective. He cries now, and I wouldn't have it any other way.

When our daughter, Josie, was born on 24 September 2020, Brendan couldn't hold it together. That made me love him a hundred times more, more than I ever thought possible. He couldn't even look at her without sobbing. He said, 'Lise, what is wrong with me?' And I said, 'Absolutely nothing, you're just in love!' He is one special man, and Josie is so lucky to have him as her 'Dadda'.

Reflect on your relationship. What do you think is the biggest strength

Lisa Smith

in your relationship? Communication? Affection? Adventure?

No colon still rollin'

Brendan knows all of me. He has seen me at my lowest of lows and highest of highs. He accepts me for all that I am and will be. Supporting every dream, I have dreamt and every idea I have thought of. Since I met Bren, I have suffered physical and emotional pain.

My health issues started early, such as bacterial meningitis, tonsilitis, and ear infections. However, as I got older, I began this strange journey of experiencing health issues that were not just the common cold, flu, or low immunity.

It started with finding out I had endometriosis and having two laparoscopies for this. I then started experiencing horrible upper abdominal pain, and, over a year, I found out I had gallstones and had my gallbladder removed.

A few years later, my sister experienced blood in her stools. Following a colonoscopy, they diagnosed her with Serrated Polyposis syndrome (SPS), resulting in the removal of her entire large intestine, a total colectomy. My brother and I both had colonoscopies on the same day because they said the syndrome was genetic.

The experts were right, and they found fifty polyps in Mitchell and 180 in me. I was twenty-five years old. My specialist encouraged me to have a total colectomy sooner rather than later. My work at the time wasn't thrilled with me having eight weeks off for recovery, so I waited eighteen months for my surgery, and on 30 November 2015, I said goodbye to my large intestine (#nocolonstillrollin).

The specialist told me the day after my surgery that they had found over 500 polyps in my large bowel, and it was a miracle none had become cancerous. Both our parents had the gene SPS. However, they were asymptomatic.

So how has losing our large intestine affected our lives, you ask? To paint a picture, I am currently sitting at a park writing this, drinking a coffee and fighting the urge to go to the toilet, and there is no toilet in sight. Other than that, our lives are completely normal. They reconnected the large bowel to the rectum, so we don't need a colostomy bag. We just go to the toilet more frequently than those with their large bowel intact. I often joke with health professionals when I'm at appointments or in the emergency department that I am an organ donor; however, there aren't too many left in my body to choose from.

Unfortunately, my issues didn't stop there. I experienced horrible pain when I was pregnant sensations of ripping, tearing, and burning as my tummy grew. Thoughts from my obstetrician, gastroenterologist and pain specialist were that some of the tissue within my abdomen was scarred.

The best way to explain this is to think of a fresh rubber band. It can be stretched quite wide with no breakage. However, think of that rubber band being in the sun or is quite old or used too often. If you stretch it too far, it will break. This is what we thought was happening inside my abdomen when Josie was growing. With the support of my pain management team, I could get through the pregnancy and make it to my C-section date.

Since the birth of our beautiful baby girl, Josie, I unfortunately still suffer from moderate to severe abdominal pain daily due to multiple abdominal surgeries. I am currently in the process of working with my pain management team to investigate what caused the pain. However, they believe the pain is related to nerve pain and nerves being trapped in my scar tissue throughout my abdomen.

So, as you can see, I've been through a lot physically and emotionally. And raising a baby whilst suffering from this type of pain has been challenging. Some days, I just feel like a failure. But, I don't want to be a weak mum or struggle to get up in the morning.

So, this is what motivates me to find out what is going on and treat it. However, I think Brendan and his mental health were overshadowed amid all of this.

What is the hardest obstacle you have overcome physically and emotionally whilst raising your child or children?

When things went from bad to worse

Bren is a fantastic dad. Even before Josie was born, we discussed our expectations of each other, and the discussions continued after her birth. I've always been open in communicating with everyone, not just Bren. Some people may say I overshare, but I like it that way.

As time went on, I started to notice Bren commenting that life just isn't the same anymore, and he wished we did more before Josie was born. He started getting frustrated with her when she cried. I'd say, 'Bren, she's a baby. That's what they do. They sometimes cry, even if we've checked off all of her needs.'

I started to notice we were fighting more, and it usually started with me being defensive of Josie when he'd get frustrated with her. After that, his sleep diminished. He'd fall asleep with no problems but woke up at waking up at 2:00 am and wouldn't get back to sleep. One morning I woke at 4:00 am, and he was gone. I called him, and he was invoicing for our plumbing business at McDonald's. After the fourth day of next to no sleep, he wasn't present and seemed to be living on auto-pilot. He had also started drinking more at night. 'Just a few beers', he'd say.

The worst day of my life

The weekend it all came out was hands down the worst weekend away of my life. I remember it like it was yesterday. We went to stay at my parent's holiday house in Noosa North Shore with some close friends. Lani and Richie have a baby, Georgie, three months younger than Josie. Lani and I decided to drive up with the girls on a Friday morning, and the boys would come together that afternoon.

Navigating Motherhood

That day I found out I was unsuccessful in securing a permanent job at QCH, and I was devastated. I just *knew* Bren would drink while Richie drove up.

I messaged him and said, 'Hey, I know you are drinking, so when you arrive, can you please just be decent to me? I found out I didn't get the job today.'

He arrived, and all hell broke loose. He was so drunk and rude. I just sobbed on Lani's shoulder for what felt like hours. I said, 'I can't do this anymore. I don't want to be with him anymore, especially like this.' I felt so hopeless, and all that security he once provided was gone.

In the morning, he apologised, and driving home, he opened his heart, and it all came out.

'I think you and Josie will be better off without me.'

'I don't want to be a dad anymore.'

'It's so hard!'

'I've sometimes thought of hurting her when I can't settle her.'

'I don't like being alone with her.'

'Life has changed so much!'

I felt my heart rip out of my chest and my stomach turn over. Then, sitting in the backseat of the car, I looked into Bren's eyes through the rear vision mirror, filled with tears, and then I looked over at Josie in her car seat, so innocent, and just cried. We both cried nearly the whole trip home.

Initially, I was angry at him and thought it was selfish. But I knew what I had to do. The mental health nurse came out, and I took a step back and pushed the personal feelings to the side.

I sat in the car and started assessing him in my head. I was thinking back to all the signs and symptoms occurring over the last eight months. Initially, I validated his feelings and told him that I thought he might be suffering from Post Natal Depression. He told me he felt a huge weight off his shoulders, having said his thoughts aloud. But then the self-loathing stepped in.

'I'm a horrible person for having these thoughts.'
'I'm such a bad Dad.'
'I feel like I've failed.'
'It's not her fault. She's just a baby.'

That night I booked Bren an appointment with his general practitioner, who diagnosed him with PND. His doctor organised a mental health care plan and suggested he see a male social worker or counsellor at the practice. Bren was also predisposed to anxiety and depression, having suffered anxiety and depression when we started our plumbing business, and was prescribed medication to manage his symptoms at that time. This time around, his doctor prescribed Metazepine to assist with sleep and anxiety because we all know four hours of sleep a night isn't sustainable. Once he began sleeping, his function in normal-daily activities improved, and he was more present. He has been seeing the counsellor every fortnight to monthly to this day.

Have you ever noticed some of these signs and symptoms in yourself or your partner?

Light at the end of the tunnel

Today, Bren is slowly returning to his normal self, feeling more confident with looking after Josie alone, adjusting to life as a dad and finding life bearable again. It makes me feel so happy to see him healthy again, and watching him with Josie brings tears to my eyes. He is the best Dad and husband, he is so helpful and proactive. I really couldn't do this without him. He works so hard for our family and comes home happy to see his baby girl and me.

So that is our story. My goal in sharing this is to raise awareness that men and their other partners *can* suffer from PND and that we always need to check in with them throughout the adjustment process of a new baby joining the family. I will finish with some ideas on preparing for a new baby and checking in with your partner. I have also included a step-by-step guide on what to do if you feel your partner is struggling with their mental health post-partum and some helpful resources.

Ensuring partners are prepared for parenthood

- Set expectations of each other.
- Communicate openly and do not demand.
- Talk to your partner about what you would like them to do to help you with the baby.
- Ask your partner how best they will remember your requests by writing a list and putting it on the fridge, having it written on their phone, or somewhere they look daily.

Encourage your partner to be as involved as possible when helping with the baby and when they've finished the task, talk about some things they could try next time and praise them on what they did well. For example, if they're burping the baby, let them work it out, and don't intervene unless they ask questions because this will make them feel inadequate.

Encourage your partner to organise social events with friends and explain how important it is for *you* to have time away from the baby.

Talk to your partner, ask how they are coping with the adjustment and encourage them to be honest. If they feel they can't speak about it, give them the option to write down their feelings.

Try not to take their feelings personally. Instead, validate them and provide reassurance.

Plan to have a date night once a month without bub.

Signs to look out for

- Depressed mood most of the day and often.
- Diminished interest or pleasure in activities.

- Not sleeping or sleeping a lot.
- Psychomotor agitation or retardation almost every day.
- Fatigue or lack of energy.
- Feelings of worthlessness or excessive or inappropriate guilt.
- Diminished ability to think or concentrate or indecisiveness.
- Increased use of alcohol or other drugs.
- Thoughts of suicide and death.
- Impatience with bub or just in general with activities.
- They avoid being alone with bub or not encouraging you to socialise.
- Isolating themselves from friends or family.
- Step-by-step guide if five or more above signs or symptoms are evident.
- Provide your partner with validation and reassurance.
- Organise them to see their doctor. Ensure you book a long appointment.

If five or more signs are evident

- Provide your partner with validation and reassurance.
- Get the doctor to prescribe a mental health care plan and refer to the appropriate counsellor or psychologist. Let your partner decide if they want to see a male or female.
- Be patient. Recovery from any mental illness takes time. Provide your partner with a safe environment at home to talk about how they're feeling.
- Don't pry following a counselling session. Let them tell you about it if they feel comfortable.
- With the consent of your partner, inform trustworthy friends and family because a good support network is crucial to recovery.

Navigating Motherhood

- Be kind and let them know how much they are valued and loved by you and bub.

Resources for extra support

- Lifeline (call 13 11 14 or chat online) https://lifeline.org.au
- Head to Health https://www.headtohealth.gov.au/
- PANDA (Perinatal Anxiety & Depression Australia) National Helpline
- 1300 726 306
- https://www.panda.org.au/images/resources-factsheets/
- Perinatal-Anxiety-and-Depression-in-Men.pdf

If you have resonated with my story and want to get in touch, please follow my Instagram: UpsideDownParenting.

Lisa Smith

Her family, friends and colleagues describe Lisa as a strong, resilient, empathetic and caring individual across all aspects of life, which is why she chose to work in a career that requires these traits. She is a Registered Nurse (Bachelor of Nursing) and Counsellor (Bachelor of Psychology Science and MHumanServ (RC)) with a passion for mental health and illness, especially in paediatrics and postpartum men or partner. Currently, she is a paediatric mental health nurse at Queensland Children's Hospital.

Lisa has a little girl, Josie, who recently turned two with her husband, Brendan. Lisa has battled with her health for a long time, both physically and emotionally, and continues to push through the pain daily to raise her beautiful daughter. She has also supported Brendan through his recovery from Post Natal Depression since Josie was seven months of age. Lisa believes PND in men and partners requires more awareness and attention.

Lisa loves spending time with family and friends, camping in their caravan and playing with their eight-month-old puppy, Maggie the Groodle.

Navigating Motherhood

Lisa's key interests in mental health care

- PND in men, partners and women.
- Paediatric mental health.
- Mental health decline linked to chronic pain sufferers.

Nina Cruz
Finding Your Magic In Motherhood

'The cave you fear to enter holds the treasure you seek.' -
Joseph Campbell

Motherhood can be a roller-coaster ride. Some days life is grand, the kids are happy, and the next moment you're down because your child is melting down, and you feel exhausted and depleted. You can go from feeling you've nailed this mothering gig to feeling overwhelmed when the chaos arrives, and it can change all in a nanosecond. From a blissful feeling to I'm ready for some me time and wondering who hears your SOS!

It can also feel like a solo journey, like you're out at sea alone and bracing for whatever the weather has in store for you. You can feel like you're paddling upstream or bobbing in the ocean and never arriving at your imagined destination. You're continually comparing your child and your parental life to the fantasy in your head.

I remember feeling this when I first became a mamma over eleven years ago. I felt intense love and joy, but I also felt overwhelmed. I felt unequipped for the task and lost my way some days. I was looking outward for answers and forgot that all my answers and treasures lay within me.

When I began to really trust myself and my inner knowing, I found those crazy parenting moments had less power over me. As I surrendered to whatever showed up, I got curious about it, and I began to stop identifying my children and my parenting moments through the lens of good or bad and right or wrong.

I could then be calm in my mothering storm and embody and hold whatever may show up within me and before me. When I became the antidote to the crazy moments, the less I felt like I was treading water and trying to stay afloat to catch my breath. When I could drop out of my head the need to fix, control, manage, change or curate what was happening on the outside, the more present I was to whatever was going on inside of me. I could then show up in the moment and be or do whatever my child or the moment required of me.

This freedom shifted my mothering, how I showed up for myself, and how I showed up for my children. With this new acceptance, and my intention to be open to all of it, even the challenging times, I found some of my most magical moments and memories were created.

'Go find yourself first so you can also find me'. - Rumi

Navigating motherhood, which is the greatest mission of a lifetime, requires you to let go of all you think you should know and instead be in tune and attuned to yourself and your child in each precious moment. It's the letting go of conditioning and the prescriptive way of how things should or shouldn't be or how our child should or shouldn't behave. Doing this allows us to show up in the moment empty, spacious and with an energy of neutrality. We are then available for whatever the moment has in store for our child and us. This is where magic is created.

The navigational system on an aeroplane plugs in a flight path before taking off into the sky. It enables the most direct path, the path of least resistance, and the fastest route to the destination. Along the way, the plane may divert around a storm or correct its course, but at all times, its focus is on the destination—where it intends to arrive.

Motherhood is like air travel. The destination is to guide our children along their path as nature intended, allowing childhood to unfold along the way. There will be bumps and unexpected turbulence, but when we stay focused on our mission as a mother, we will navigate these moments from a place of love and compassion. We will surrender and be non-resistant to whatever path we must take with our child or whatever detour may be in store on our journey together.

We always have a choice regarding how we travel and how we want to show up for our child, even when it appears there is no choice. We may be attached to one way or believe there is a right way. Often, we can get in the way of all the possibilities available to our child and us because we are so fixated on how it should be.

We are cut off from our own sense of inner knowing, our internal guidance system.

We are cut off because we are conditioned to think there is a right or wrong way.

'Out beyond ideas of wrongdoing and right doing, there is a field. I'll meet you there.' - Rumi

When the navigational system on an aeroplane is lost, it's flying blindly in the sky. It loses its tracking system and can no longer stay on its intended path. So likewise, when we lose our sense of inner guidance, we rely solely on external information to guide us. We also lose our inner foresight about what we intuitively feel is best for ourselves and our children.

In my early days as a mamma, I was swept up in taking action 'doing' on the outside. I tried to know it all and find solutions, but I became lost and confused at times and 'busy', not always knowing what was best for myself and my child.

It was exhausting, overwhelming and confusing. When you rely on the external for the answers, you can feel drained because you give your power and energy away to everything on the outside. As a result, you don't feel empowered as a parent and can feel anxious and fearful that you're making the wrong choices and decisions. This is because the answers are not coming from within.

Mothering from your greatness

Greatness lives inside us all—a spark, a light that guides us along the path of our highest good. Our children also have this inbuilt system, and the greatest gift we can give them is to trust our own guidance and allow them to trust theirs.

> 'Knowing yourself is the gateway to understanding and knowing your child.'
> - Nina Cruz

From my experience coaching mammas and also being a Mamma myself, I've found we all truly want the best for our children and want to be the best mamma we can be.

To move away from the fear and control parenting paradigm of previous generations, doing the inner work and looking in the mirror is pivotal. Knowing yourself is the gateway to becoming the best mamma for yourself and your child.

> 'Compassion is knowing our darkness enough so we can sit in the dark with others.' - Brene Brown

Tapping into your own intuition and being led by the information you receive is powerful. Taking the next most obvious step that is received by

Nina Cruz

you is all that is required. So often, we seek answers all over the place and miss what is right before us, blatantly obvious, as we get so caught up in our heads. It then becomes difficult to see the truth.

The parenting game changes when we begin to play by our own rules and no longer follow the prescribed parenting path. This allows us to gain clarity and simplicity and allows us to hear and listen with our hearts. When we know what truly matters, that our children desire to be seen by us, heard by us, and know they matter to us, it really doesn't have to be so complicated. Now that doesn't mean you'll tick each box at every moment. We are human, and there is no such thing as perfect parenting, but when we are aware of our sacred duty and can bring our focus to it each day, parenting becomes easier.

My children, Jakob and Kira, are my greatest teachers, and I continue to learn and grow with their daily lessons. The lessons have been profound, complex, tough and sometimes hard to swallow. Navigating my parenting journey in the early days felt like I jumped on a roller-coaster ride I wasn't strapped in for. It was full of ups and downs, like someone else controlled the navigational instruments.

Now, after years of learning and growing and re-learning, then unlearning and growing some more, I can understand why, with compassion, I was the way I was and why I experienced motherhood the way I did at the start.

Understanding myself, my patterns, and my egoic agendas has been the gateway to self-acceptance and freedom. Choosing to create beyond my conditioning and childhood patterns has been powerful. It's what I love supporting parents to do—empowering parents so they can raise empowered children. We all have genius locked inside of us. It's time to bring the inside out!

> *'Every interaction with our child is a reflection of our own relationship with ourselves.'* - Dr Shefali Tsabary

'What you resist persists'

'What you resist persists' is a term coined by the renowned psychiatrist Carl Yung. This means that whatever we resist, we bring closer to us and create it because we are so focused on it. I constantly tried to fix and change what was happening in my early parenting years. Rarely did I accept the as-is. And what happened? I just got more of what I was resisting! Focus is certainly our superpower as parents, and our focus is creating our experience as a mother.

'Outward change comes after we change from within.' - Bob Proctor

Nowadays, I absolutely love to support parents in accepting where they are in their parenting journey. You don't have to love it or like it. You just have to stop fighting it and then focus on what you desire to create for yourself and your children. It's from the place of surrender you can stop giving your power and focus to the things you don't want to happen or that are happening or could happen. Then, you can completely shift your focus towards what you *really* want. It's magical to witness the freedom that comes when we stop giving our power to all the problems we think the ego thinks we need to fix. And what happens? They dissolve like magic!

You shift your focus, and in the process, how you see your child shifts in miraculous ways!

'While the days of parenting may seem so long, the years are so short.'
- Dr Daniel Siegel

From navigating my parenting journey, I have realised some truths that I hold firmly planted in the garden of my mind. Because I know very well these moments with my children in their childhood are fleeting and will never come again. This focus pulls me into line, and I have learnt to harness and bring out the goodness in each moment. Sometimes I nail it, and other times I get stuck in my mind trying to curate and dictate all the *shoulds*. My ego tries to swoop in and tarnish the moment that robs my children and me of the magic.

You see, the ego is our protective shell. It's constantly trying to keep us safe and certain. However, it's navigating from our past experiences and isn't rooted in our current reality. So we need to shift our focus to what we intend for the moment.

Thankfully it's a skill we can all learn in order to redirect our focus and stop believing and then playing out these thoughts and patterns that aren't real and are based on our past experiences and biases. What you focus on grows, and what you put your attention on expands. What you water, nourish and nurture will thrive.

Here are eight magical Mamma truths I know that can support you in navigating your mothering journey with more creativity, connectivity, intuition and fun!

- Know yourself because self-awareness is the key. Parenting is all about you! So when you 'think' it's about your child, turn the spotlight back on yourself and ask, 'What is going on inside of me? What is my child teaching me about me?'
- Find your point of reference and yourself, 'Where are you now in the chaos and overwhelming feelings of motherhood?' Be with the resistance you may feel right now, wherever you are in your current mamma reality. Accept it, then look at what kind of mamma you want to be. What do you want to create? Then redirect your energy towards that commitment. You're creating your child's childhood memories.
- There is nothing to fix, and you're not broken. You're a divine Mamma. You are whole, and you were divinely picked to parent your child. Remember this.

- Your focus is your super-mama power. Decide what you want to focus on. You always have a choice, so choose wisely. Become aware of where you are truly placing your focus because this has the power and is creating your mothering experience.
- Be the observer. When you're observing, you're no longer playing out the pattern. You are the awareness observing the pattern. This is powerful. This is power. This is freedom.
- Tap into your silly, playful side. The sillier, the better.

I guarantee you that everything is better when you add a sprinkle of silliness, fun and playfulness to the moment. Your child will be putty in your hands. They'll surprise you and do more of what you want them to do. They'll want more of the funny mamma moments if you connect to the playfulness within and express it in the resistant moments with your child. Play is the language of childhood. Play is the ultimate connector to our children.

Most of the magic moments I've spontaneously created with my children are when I've gotten out of my own way. They're born from their resistance to doing something, not from planning an incredible outing together. No, they're born from challenge and resistance that, in actuality, is creative energy. I have spent a good portion of forty-plus years avoiding conflict. When I began to lean in and not fight or try to avoid or resolve this resistance or conflict when I began to tap into this energy, magic happened! But I had to be willing to let go big time. Let go of controlling or avoiding what was happening or trying to improve things.

I had to be with it all and not go into rescuing myself or my children from what was unfolding in the sibling fights, upsets, meltdowns, chaos, drama, resistance or any other uncomfortable dilemmas of motherhood. Also, I had to hold the intention of what I wanted to create with my children first in my mind's eye. Even when, in reality, I saw the opposite of my desired vision. I have blindfolded my kids to get them to brush their teeth. I've given toothbrushes up a tree, grabbed the broom and played limbo and given pony rides. I've allowed my son to move furniture safely to make cubby houses. I've learnt to get out of the way when my kids are playing together. Even if this means they're re-arranging the house in the process. I've learnt to let go and flow and allow space for whatever needs to be birthed in the moment.

- What you think is important is not important. Thinking is the problem. The logical mind is a program conditioned by our childhood experiences. It keeps us stuck in the past, creating new experiences via past thinking. It keeps us stuck as parents. Your child is begging for you to be here now not in your head, thinking, planning or organising. Your children are saying, 'Be here, Mama?' 'Hold my hand, Mama?' 'See the wondrous-magical world I see, Mama.' 'Don't miss the moment, Mama!'
- Here is a powerful reminder—you can't go back to your child's childhood ever again! So don't miss these precious moments!
- Make it up! You don't need to know it all! Be a child, and make it up!
- Do the nonsensical. Let your imagination run wild like your child.

'Give the ones you love wings to fly, roots to come back, and reasons to stay.' -
Dalai Lama

Remember, you're a powerful Mamma. You are whole, worthy, and behind the wheel, navigating your own unique mothering journey. Tap into and use your own navigational system because it will steer you and your child to create a magical childhood together!

'That was her magic—she could still see the sunset, even on those darkest days.'
- Atticus

Nina Cruz

Are you ready to dive deeper and begin navigating your parenting journey feeling more empowered and guided by your intuition?

Want to know more about conscious parenting and how to be an empowered Mamma and consciously create your mothering journey?

Nina Lives in Sydney, Australia, with her two amazing and incredibly wise teachers, Jakob and Kira, and their dogs, Jakson and Luna. Nina is on a mission to support parents to become empowered and create the parenting experience they truly desire for themselves and their children.

She has a private coaching practice offering individual and group coaching programs on conscious, empowered parenting and conscious creation. She also runs an intensive six-month program that focuses on becoming the predominant creator in your life.

Nina Cruz is a certified Conscious Parent Coach/Social Worker and Meditation Teacher whose mission is to support parents in building healthy connections with their children. She does this by teaching them conscious and empowered parenting, so they can consciously raise empowered children.

When a parent's inner world shifts, their outer world changes, transforming the parent-child dynamic from chaos to control to worth and connection.

Parents who gain a new sense of awareness through inner transformation create a new blueprint for themselves and their children. This is why one of Nina's greatest passions is to guide parents to do their own 'inner work' so their children can be free to live out their authentic destinies.

Certified as a Conscious Parenting Coach, Nina integrates eastern mindfulness, western psychology and ancient wisdom in helping parents no longer live out their ancestral legacies and tap into their own inner knowing. Her expertise has allowed her to collaborate with experts around the globe.

Connect with Nina

Connect and work with Nina so that you can be a part of the conscious and empowered parenting movement and benefit your child and your life in magical ways.

Wild Network Channel:
http://bit.ly/NinaCruzCoach
Instagram: @ninacruzcoach
Facebook: @ninacruzconsciouscoaching, https://www.facebook.com/ninacruzconsciouscoaching/
Website: https://ninacruzconsciouscoaching.com/
(to book your Free Discovery Session with Nina, go to her website)
Download a free 12 Days of Presence Program:
https://ninacruzconsciouscoaching.com/free-offers/
– Twelve days to become a more present parent
https://instagram.com/ninacruzcoach?r=nametag

www.ingramcontent.com/pod-product-compliance
Lightning Source LLC
Chambersburg PA
CBHW020322010526
44107CB00054B/1942